LEADING
from the
HEART

Lifetime Reflections on Spiritual Development

Robert Boyd Munger
with Robert C. Larson

InterVarsity Press
Downers Grove, Illinois

InterVarsity Press® is the book-publishing division of InterVarsity Christian Fellowship®, a student movement active on campus at hundreds of universities, colleges and schools of nursing in the United States of America, and a member movement of the International Fellowship of Evangelical Students. For information about local and regional activities, write Public Relations Dept., InterVarsity Christian Fellowship, 6400 Schroeder Rd., P.O. Box 7895, Madison, WI 53707-7895.

All Scripture quotations, unless otherwise indicated, are taken from the HOLY BIBLE, NEW INTERNATIONAL VERSION®. NIV®. Copyright © 1973, 1978, 1984 by International Bible Society. Used by permission of Zondervan Publishing House. All rights reserved.

ISBN 0-8308-1613-5

Printed in the United States of America ∞

Library of Congress Cataloging-in-Publication Data

Munger, Robert Boyd, 1910-
    Leading from the heart: lifetime reflections on spiritual
development/Robert Boyd Munger; with Robert C. Larson.
        p.   cm.
    Includes bibliographical references.
    ISBN 0-8308-1613-5 (pbk.: alk. paper)
    1. Munger, Robert Boyd, 1910-   2. Presbyterian churches—
Clergy—Biography.   3. Christian leadership.   4. Spiritual
formation.   I. Larson, Robert C.   II. Title.
BX7260.M79A3   1995
285.8'092—dc20
    [B]   95-38607
                                                                                        CIP

18	17	16	15	14	13	12	11	10	9	8	7	6	5	4	3	2	1
10	09	08	07	06	05	04	03	02	01	00	99	98	97	96	95		

Acknowledgments

Through the efforts of many people, this book has finally become a reality. I first want to acknowledge my debt of gratitude to the members of the Disciples, a Sunday-morning Bible class of the Lake Avenue Congregational Church in Pasadena, California, for their supportive interest and practical response. After listening to me as their Bible teacher each week for three years and hearing about the book I was "one day" going to write, they put me on the line and said, "Now go and do it!"

I want to thank the instigators of the project, Bob Oberlander and Bob Harris, for their help in enlisting the interest of the members of the class. I also want to express special thanks to Roland Hinz, who believed in me enough to invest his support and encouragement. Deep thanks also go to Dr. Cliff Penner, who gave generously of his wise counsel and experience.

I have learned much about spiritual growth and leadership from the young people in my various pastorates. To other special friends who for many years urged and encouraged me to write, my special thanks.

To my "covenant brothers," a group of pastors with whom I have been meeting regularly for twenty-five years, I owe a great debt of gratitude, as I have seen them model spiritual leadership at its best. And most of all, I want to thank the students at Fuller Theological Seminary for what I learned about the formation of spiritual leadership from them in the ten years I taught there.

Thanks, too, to those in administration at Fuller Theological Seminary, who in my retirement years provided me with office space and the freedom to minister to students both one-to-one and in small groups. This gave me the opportunity to encourage them as they were continuing their spiritual journey in a seminary setting.

This book would not have been possible without the creative efforts of Robert C. Larson, my coauthor, with whom I have spent many hours sharing and sharpening my thinking. Bob spent months organizing and integrating volumes of material into what has become a readable and coherent whole. I also owe a debt of gratitude to my wife, Edie, who worked with Bob in line editing to give the manuscript the authenticity of my thinking.

I am grateful to Barbara Friend, who transcribed many long hours of taped material into a workable manuscript for editing. To so many dear friends I give my heartfelt thanks.

PROLOGUE
Lessons
in Spiritual
Navigation

The world is desperately crying for leaders. I have written this book with that universal need in mind. The words that follow are for people who have the conviction, character and courage to transcend self-interest and stand for what is true, just and merciful. Men and women everywhere are asking: *Where—and who—are our leaders? Who will provide us with a map and a compass to get us out of our present mess and move us into the light?*

Around the world, the role of leaders is changing in the face of growing expectations and cries for accountability. Robin Wright, describing "the leadership revolution," wrote in the *Los Angeles Times* (January 19, 1993): "The most significant change in leadership stems from shifts emanating not from the top or even the middle but from the bottom: Leadership is evolving foremost because power is spreading."

The everyday Christians I associate with constantly remind me that leadership is what the church is all about. Not necessarily a professional, highly trained, theologically qualified leadership, as important as that may be. Rather, a leadership that *leads from below,* that understands its profound role as servant, that knows how to listen and respond to the real needs of real people. The church today needs leaders who demonstrate the capacity to communicate and live the good news so there is no question as to where their loyalties lie.

A leadership of personal integrity, a commitment to Jesus Christ—not just to programs *about* Jesus Christ—and an uncompromising allegiance to the gospel are the only dynamics that will ever give the church the power to be the driving force needed as we approach the unbelievable challenges of a new millennium. Like it or not, understand it or not, and even if you've heard it before and are tired of hearing it, we are in a fierce battle, not against flesh and blood but against powers and principalities. This is not an enemy we can line up in the cross hairs of our physical weapons. Our adversary is an invisible foe that's creating visible consequences. This war is over the questions *Whose values will we take as our own? Whom do we follow? How do we sift the true from the false, the leader from the charlatan?* The battle lines are being drawn deep in the hearts and souls of men, women, boys and girls as never before in history.

Ed Hayes, president of the Baptist Seminary in Denver, Colorado, says, in his insightful pamphlet "The Cultural War: Seizing the Opportunity,"

> The real question in the fading twilight of the 20th Century is, "Whose values will prevail?" There is a cultural war going on in America. We are witnessing a gradual abdication of the traditional underpinning of American society. . . . In reality it is a battle about matters of the spirit. Christians call it spiritual warfare. . . . [That's why] we must return to the springs of living water. This is exactly what Jesus offered the Samaritan woman.

It is folly simply to wring our hands at the moral dilemma facing us. We must do more than lament that our precious values are being "devalued." This is the hour for leadership at every level—government, family, university, seminary and the church—to return to those springs of living water that will give us the courage and the nerve to speak the truth, thus providing us with the guidance we desperately need as we voyage into the stormy seas that lie ahead.

We are in a leadership crisis. We see it not only in the church but also among Christian men and women who are trying to fight the battle in the secular world. People with a passion for moral responsibility are longing for leadership. But how to produce great leaders seems to elude us in our enlightened late twentieth century. We need to remember that true leadership is a gift from God—therefore we need to produce *godly* men and women. We may have a poverty of leadership in our own country, but as one scans the world horizon we are seeing a remarkable explosion of faith and life overseas with increasing numbers of Christian leaders at the helm. Stories of faith and confidence in the living God are found all over this planet. Christ is alive in the Two-Thirds World, and his messengers are more eager to share the good news than at any time in those nations' history. Perhaps this is the time for us to turn to our brothers and sisters overseas and ask *them* to come over into Macedonia to help *us!*

At the turn of this century, thousands of eager students were motivated to serve Christ in other lands through the Student Volunteer Movement, one of the great missionary movements of history with world-influencing, life-changing impact. In *The Future Leadership of the Church,* John R. Mott called for spiritual leaders who would "leave a message and be conscious of a mission," be able "effectively to express this passion for Christ and people" and above all be "great in character."

Thousands of eager students responded to Mott's challenge and followed their Lord as missionaries through what became the Student Volunteer Movement. These many decades later, the cause of Christ continues to advance, most remarkably in the Two-Thirds World and in the developing countries where earnest Christians are charting their own spiritual course through dangerous, difficult waters. Faithful servants of Christ in places like China, the former USSR, the nations of

Africa, the Middle East, southeast Asia and the countries of Latin America have a message, a mission and a passion for Christ. Their passion is stirred by the light of God; their mission is reflected in the face of Jesus; and their message is a love for people without Christ. The hearts of these believers are inflamed as they stand humbly at the foot of his cross.

Thank God for the work of Mott and so many of those early student missionaries who put down such deep, solid roots that continue to produce a rich harvest in the lands beyond the sea. But what about here at home? Is it possible for us to recapture our own vision for a message and a mission? Is it possible for us again to focus on the serious development of a Christian leadership that stands up for what is right, that refuses to compromise, that will lead fearlessly, and that will demonstrate the commitment to help us turn the tide of unbridled secularism to an unashamed declaration of faith in Jesus Christ? My faith-bound answer is *Yes, I know we can if we will let him!*

While I have opportunity, I want to share some of the things I am learning about God's ways of maturing and training for Christian leaders. Jesus Christ himself is the source of our Christian message and mission. In the training of the Twelve he has given us his method for reproducing his character and ministry in ordinary people. It is a process of spiritual formation that offers the key to producing truly spiritual leaders. Spiritual formation means learning to rely on the living Lord who is with us in both victories and defeats. It means becoming mature as Christians—shifting the weight of confidence from ourselves and our abilities to the Savior who has taken upon himself responsibility for our lives. Spiritual formation is response to the ultimate reality, living by faith with our living Lord.

I am encouraged that many seminaries have begun to offer courses in spiritual formation, encouraging students preparing for ministry to create space for the liberating power of the Holy Spirit in their innermost selves. It was during a time of discouragement in the early years of my first pastorate that this liberating power of the Holy Spirit became real to me and changed the direction of my life and ministry. My cold heart became a burning heart, and I made the decision to be guided by that vision rather than my own ambition and need to be successful. I began to learn what it means to lead from the heart.

Life is difficult and complicated, and so is spiritual leadership. What I have learned and am still learning is from the heart. I have learned that the way to the heart is the way to freedom, because it is the way to truth. Henri Nouwen expresses it succinctly when he says, "Spiritual formation gives us a free heart able to see the face of God in the midst of a hardened world, and allows us to use our skills to make that face visible to all who live in darkness" (*Sojourners*, August 1977, p. 16).

This is the kind of leadership our world cries out for. My purpose in this book is to pass on to you what I have seen God do for those to whom he has given the purpose, passion and power to fulfill the most important mission on earth.

Pollster George Gallup gives his own prescription for what is needed in the 1990s—a decade he refers to as one of "deepening commitment." Leaders, he says, need to listen, teach, encourage, inspire and target key groups for spiritual nourishment.

Are you ready for such training? Are you prepared to let God grow you into a leader who will help do battle with the cultural-spiritual war that needs to be fought at every level of our society? If so, perhaps the words of this manual may indeed become a navigational guide to help you chart the waters of your own development as a Christian leader.

Let me say that I am just a fellow struggler, sharing my thoughts with you who, I hope, are also struggling to be the person and leader God wants you to be. During my years of ministry as a pastor, teacher and player-coach, there have been times when I thought I knew something about the game of Christian leadership, only to discover I was still a beginner.

So I will not use these pages to frustrate myself by dwelling on opportunities missed or perspectives muddled. Instead, I'm writing this book because I am grateful to my Captain for a life of limitless blessing and intimate friendships in what has become a journey with all the storms, harbors, near-shipwrecks, mutinies and on-board training that come with any decent voyage.

One of my favorite mentors on this journey of discovery has been Henrietta Mears, Christian leader and Bible teacher extraordinaire at Hollywood Presbyterian Church from 1928 to 1963. As Henrietta looked into the eyes of her college Bible class students, she would often say something like "I'm excited for you. You have a wonderful Savior, and with him you're going to do great things for God." Her enthusiasm said to me, *I'm here to help you, pray for you and stand by you as you discover and do the will of God.* How could any student not feel special with such an outpouring of praise, encouragement and affection?

Although I was not in her college class, I still consider her my mentor and guide, one for whom I have often been grateful during the subsequent years of my ministry as pastor and teacher—and even now as a writer of the book you hold in your hands.

So why do I write this book, especially when there are already plenty of volumes on leadership? I want to share with you what to me have become simple, time-tested principles of spiritual navigation and spiritual development. You may be a "novice seaman," learning the ropes, just figuring out what it takes to be a decent deck hand. Or you may be an "old salt" with many voyages, battle scars and skirmishes behind you. Whoever you are and wherever you are in your spiritual journey, it is my prayer that this manual of spiritual navigation may serve as a compass for you on your own pilgrimage.

First I will tell you my story, because my confidence comes initially through my own experience.

My pilgrimage began one stormy night crossing the Pacific as a college student. An encounter with the possibility of death sent me in search of God, and I discovered Jesus, the Friend who promised to shed light in the midst of my confusion.

After a frustrating year of living in two worlds, I learned that my Friend also meant to be my Captain in the voyage of life. I set off to Bible school and then seminary to master the fundamentals of spiritual life and leadership. I offer the experiences and lessons of this early journey in the first four chapters of this book, as the foundation for the years of ministry that followed.

I learned the art of pastoring in a small church in South Hollywood, California, where I discovered how the Holy Spirit could empower a dynamic ministry. Nine years later, I found the heart of my ministry in Berkeley, where a vital congregation in the university environment was strategically placed to make its mark on the world. The 1960s found me in a Seattle church, struggling with the social upheaval of the time but learning about Christian community. Finally, at Fuller Seminary I began to share the lessons of spiritual formation learned along the way with a new generation of people preparing for ministry.

In chapter five I will talk about where the power for this ministry comes from and how it comes. Then we will look at our missionary mandate and how it is to be lived out (chapter six)—all of this in the context of community (chapter seven). The crucial concept of teaming will be the subject of chapter eight.

The journey I describe in the chapters of this book is offered to you as an encouragement for your own journey. It all started as an exciting adventure, the opportunity of a lifetime for a young junior from UC Berkeley to ship out from the safe harbors of routine living and launch into a world of the unexplored and unknown. The date was summer 1931. The place: the South Pacific. The weather: typhoon conditions. Visibility: zero.

1
Light:
The Journey
Begins

LIVE IN PEACE YOURSELF

AND THEN YOU CAN BRING

PEACE TO OTHERS.

Thomas à Kempis, *The Imitation of Christ*

I t was a seven-thousand-ton ship, one of the smallest of the Matson line. Not very big by today's standards. It carried only first-class passengers, a limited number in steerage, and some freight. It was so old that this was to be its next-to-last run between San Francisco and Sydney, Australia, with stops in Honolulu, Samoa and Fiji.

It was the summer before my senior year at Berkeley, and my closest fraternity brother and I were ready to see the world for two months. We signed up as cadets and were put to work doing everything but the glamorous jobs. Still, this was adventure, wasn't it? For a twenty-year-old college kid who had never ventured beyond the Golden Gate, the turn-of-the century vessel seemed like an ocean liner.

I thought I'd seen weather in Berkeley. But compared to what I experienced one dark, cold night in the South Pacific en route home from Sydney to San Francisco, the most severe Bay Area weather amounted to little more than a drizzle.

It was my watch, and my job was to tour the ship and punch the time-clock stations. The sea was raging. I couldn't believe waves could be so many stories high. They were monsters, and the bigger they got, the smaller I felt. More than once I asked myself, *Why did I talk myself into taking this trip?* My mind raced back to the comforts of home and my brothers at the fraternity at UC Berkeley. But no, that would have been too easy. I'd wanted to prove something to myself. I'd wanted adventure. Well, now I had adventure, and it was spelled T-Y-P-H-O-O-N, and I didn't much like the looks of it.

A Raging Sea

Being assaulted by winds and walls of waves on a wildly tossing sea was like being run over by a train in a dark tunnel. We knew the typhoon was coming, but I, for one, hadn't expected it to pack such a wallop. Everything was battened down as we prepared to take a direct hit. Those of us who were on deck had our slickers on, similar to the old yellow slickers used by New England fishermen. Being a novice to things of the sea, I'd hung mine up near a hot pipe in the fo'c's'le a few days before, and the heat had melted all the oil from the fabric. Now my slicker leaked like a sieve. It wasn't much good, but it was all I had to wear as the ship shuddered and pitched into huge mountains of brine and foam.

It was fast approaching midnight. As I made my final rounds on deck, everything I saw brought on physical terror. The lights of the ship re-flected only a few feet out over the water, so each wave became visible only as it reared to crash. More than once I thought, *What if I were washed overboard while making my rounds? No one would even know. I'd be lost forever in a violent, angry sea.* The possibility of death was enough to focus my mind. But almost as terrifying as drowning was the fear of falling into darkness and death all alone—no one to see, hear or report the blotting out of a life.

I went below to steerage, right by the rudder. There the steerage passengers clustered. It was an area just for men. Instead of bunks they slept on boards, rather like pieces of shelving, about eighteen inches wide with six-inch upright planks as dividers. The boards were set up eight across and three deep. Those were close quarters. The steerage passengers were mostly Malaysians who had already been thrust into crosscultural trauma. Now the pitching and rolling of the ship and the deafening roar of the grinding rudder-control machinery, punctuated by an explosive banging of the rudder itself, were enough to unnerve the stoutest heart. Some twenty-five men clung to one another in a tight bundle of fear and panic.

In steerage, as the bow of the ship pitched deep, the propeller would come right up out of the water with a terrifying roar and vibrate the entire stern of the vessel as though it were coming apart at the seams. (That in itself should have been enough to prompt a conversion experience for me!) The men were being thrown back and forth on each other so fiercely that at one point they looked like the mob of baseball players who rush out of the dugout and pile on the pitcher after he strikes out the last batter to win the final game of the World Series.

Facing Death

I was still on duty, responsible to make hourly rounds of the ship and punch the time clock. So I struggled to make it back to the bridge. To get there I had to climb the rigging that angled to the mast, where I bypassed the boat deck by about three inches. That got me by the first-class cabins on the middle deck, which I mounted by swinging from the rail to the seaside. Then I had to drop from the rigging to the deck. Always this move had to be in sync with the pitch of the ship as it rocked back and forth and up and down. The idea was to jump off the rigging onto the deck as the ship leaned toward the opposite side, so I could drop straight down.

The maneuver called for care even in smooth waters. But during the storm the real art was to hang on the slippery, varnished rope ladder and climb twenty feet of rigging as it slanted out over the water with the roll of the ship.

Going up the ladder, my body was tight with tension. I knew if I didn't hang on, I'd be gone and would not be missed until the watch was over. As I meditated on that possibility and looked through the rungs of the rope ladder right down into the turbulent sea, my climb seemed to last forever. Finally I let go and dropped to the deck. But because I was tense with fear, I tried to move too quickly on the wet, slick, canvas-covered surface. I slipped and fell, spread-eagle. Then I felt myself beginning to slide.

The soles of my tennis shoes couldn't get a purchase on the wet canvas. The edge of the deck was smooth and rounded so that lifeboats would swing out freely. I tried to dig my fingernails into the top of the deck, but to no avail. I just kept slipping back toward the water. I could feel myself going overboard. I couldn't stop. My mind raced with images of Munger dropping, engulfed by the waters of an angry sea, lost forever in the cold, dark night.

After what seemed like an eternity, the ship finally rocked in the opposite direction. I struggled to my knees—I couldn't get my legs to do much more than that. Somehow I managed to make it to the postage-stamp-sized housing behind the smokestack, where the telegraph operator's hut squatted. Exhausted, I collapsed in a heap with my back propped against the wall.

Ten or twelve minutes later, I finally found the strength to stagger back to my watch. I felt I'd had enough adventure to last a lifetime.

Seeking the Meaning of Life

For many nights after that terrifying storm, I found myself standing watch under the stars and wondering, *What is the meaning of existence, anyway? Am I anything but a zero in the midst of millions of other zeros?*

If I'd been lost at sea, would I have fulfilled any purpose? Would my life have been worth anything? Deep inside, I knew my loss would not have made even the slightest dent in history.

My thoughts continued. *What if I survive this voyage and live a long, useful life? Even then will my life have any ultimate significance or meaning?* I answered no to that also.

Emotionally and spiritually I felt I was lost in a sea of meaninglessness, drowning in a vast vacuum of emptiness. The more I thought about my situation, the deeper was my depression.

I began to compare myself with the members of the crew. I figured that with my pedigree and behavior, I was certainly better than they were. After all, some of them were existing at a subhuman level. They were living solely for creature comforts and animal appetites; all they seemed to want was lots of liquor and women and enough money to buy them. Just hearing their constant strings of four-letter words made me feel seasick.

But was my motivation in life much better? Was I not existing for my own creature comforts, which would ultimately make my life as valueless as theirs? Sure, my tastes were more refined, but that didn't mean much. I kept asking myself, *Munger, how are you really any different from those men who seem to live at an animal level?*

For three years I'd been trying to have fun fraternity-style. I would often escort a date to San Francisco on the car ferry and spend a lot of my hard-earned money taking her to a hotel for a long night of dancing. We'd then head back across the bay to Berkeley, continuing our conversation and gazing at the stars shining over Twin Peaks, or sitting in the car and being romantic. But now none of that even seemed remotely important. Nothing I was doing was taking me anywhere. I knew there must be an answer for me, but I was hard-pressed to find it.

Here I was, returning from Australia—same stars, different waters. I'd seen a bit of the world and would bring home plenty of good memories. Still, I was just as disillusioned and disturbed as I'd been back at Berkeley. Would I ever find an answer to the depression that dogged me?

Looking for Answers

Two weeks after my narrow escape at sea, I found myself once again on watch in the middle of the night. Again I was alone, but this time the seas were calm and the stars so bright I felt I could touch them. I knew that for centuries seafarers had set their clocks on the movements of the same stars I saw scattered throughout the universe. I couldn't help but compare the ordered movement of the stars, the planets and the galaxies millions of light-years away with the chaos and meaningless-ness of my life, so full of pain and disappointment.

What was the answer? I had received all the opportunities in the world to position myself for success: a good university education, a caring family, lots of friends. Yet my life was still without any real interest or purpose.

My Christian background told me that if there was an answer, it would come in affirming Jesus Christ as Savior and Lord. From day one I had heard sermons from the pulpit and advice from my parents that ex-pounded on my need for a personal relationship with God through his Son. It all sounded good, but I wasn't convinced it would work.

As I thought about this a few night watches later, something strange began to come over me. I was being washed with a new reality. My clamlike heart was slowly being pried open by something greater than myself. That's when I prayed, "Christ, if you're real, if you're there, if there's any meaning at all in this great universe for human life, then make yourself known. If you're up there, if you're the living God, and if you can make the stars move so smoothly and accurately that we can set our clocks by them century after century, you surely must have a way of communicating yourself." It was my first real prayer.

Then, without warning, the truth of Christ came to me . . . *I am the light of the world.*

I responded, "If you really are light, let me see some of it, and I'll try to follow it!" That was the moment I opened the door of my heart to Christ. I didn't know it, but all along I had been longing desperately for the light.

Head vs. Heart Knowledge

Why do I tell this personal story? Because we all come to Christ through *a unique self-disclosure of God.* For me it started with terror at sea—there I confronted my meaningless self. For you it will be different (at least I hope so). But the gospel message is always clear: there's no way you and I can get to God through our own efforts. We can't climb a ladder and finally get over the top to see the light. It will always be a revelation. It's like getting to know a friend. You may know something *about* the person, but until that individual reveals himself or herself, you never really *know* your new acquaintance.

Over the years I'd tucked away a lot of information about God. I had a deep respect for his handiwork in creation. I had heard the gospel stories about Jesus and the wonders of God. But I had no relationship with the Creator. It was all theory. It was as if I had been parading through a dark room crowded with large pieces of ornate furniture and delicate vases. I was knocking everything over and making a royal mess of it. Then I stumbled toward the light switch and turned it on. Suddenly the room—and my life—was flooded with light. My world finally began to make sense. I started to see things as God meant them to be.

"Nothing Religious, Please . . ."

By the time I'd returned to home port in San Francisco weeks later, the earnestness of my cry had dimmed, quickly crowded out by the fun of telling old friends and associates about my exciting journey. It was easy for me to talk about the adventure; I couldn't—I wouldn't—talk about my prayer. Even though I knew I needed God's light to shed its brilliance on the shadows of my life, I refused to respond. I was still taking it all in—but choosing not to commit myself to follow through on what

I'd thought and prayed during the storm at sea.

I had hardly regained my shore legs when my parents told me that they were headed for a two-week vacation at Mount Hermon, a well-known Christian conference center nestled in the Santa Cruz Mountains. I said I'd go with them on one condition: I would spend no time learning about God. I reminded them that I had just returned from a two-month voyage and needed a few days of vacation.

I remember telling my mother, "I'll come down to Mount Hermon, but don't expect me to go to anything religious." I knew a conference was being held on the grounds, and I wasn't about to get involved. But Mother was smart. She'd been praying for years for her wandering son. She knew I was in the fraternity crowd and had zero interest in church. She also knew I had some reservations about Christians—I stereotyped them as a crowd that didn't know how to have fun, social misfits, unpopular throwaways who'd been left behind.

I had what today we'd call an attitude. When I did go to church once in a while with my parents, I would hear myself saying in my head, *Hey, Lord, take notice here—Munger's in church today. Cross off some of the bad marks, and put some checks on the good side of the ledger.* God certainly must have been impressed.

That was how I felt when I arrived at Mount Hermon, and my mother knew it. So she decided to do a little parental manipulating, first by reintroducing me to a family friend, an attractive young woman I'd not seen for years but with whom I'd spent some happy times on several family occasions.

Marian Parish was still a lot of fun. What I hadn't expected was that Marian also belonged to an enthusiastic group of Christian young people who had come to a conference at Mount Hermon with Henrietta Mears, teacher of their college class at Hollywood Presbyterian Church.

Before I knew it, Marian had introduced me to a few of her girlfriends. I liked that—a lot! Many of these young women were lovely, but that wouldn't have been necessary: after two months at sea, a petticoat draped on a telephone pole would have looked pretty good to me.

Later in the week I found myself alone with one of these attractive young women. I asked her if she'd like to go to a movie in Santa Cruz. Her face lit up, and I thought, *Boy, this is going to be great!* Then she popped my balloon by saying, "I'd love to, but I'm with the conference and I can't go with you tonight. Why don't you come with me, and then maybe we could do something afterwards?"

Fading Prejudice

I figured I had nothing to lose. In fact, spending a few minutes hearing about God might even pay off with an enjoyable summer relationship. I'd already decided we would sit in the back row, close to the nearest exit. But my friend insisted, "I want you to come with our gang."

I thought, *Why not?* After all, there were a number of other attractive young women in the group. So I found myself in the second row, jammed in with a bunch of students waiting to hear Henrietta speak. I didn't have a chance!

Here I was confronted with something I'd never seen before. These kids looked good and were dressed to the nines. They knew how to socialize and were comfortable having a good time. My prejudices against Christians started fading fast as I found myself attending the meetings night after night—and enjoying it. I even started listening to the messages.

The last night of the conference, the group gathered in a semicircle of bleachers overlooking an inspiring vista of majestic mountain red-woods framed by a beautiful evening sky. In that "victory circle" many of my new friends began to give fervent testimony to what Christ had done in their lives. Some of what I heard that night was hype and emotion; but a lot of it was also straight from the heart. I was starting to get the message that there was a key to a life-changing reality. They were talking about real happiness, fulfillment, having a life worth living. Many of them seemed to know Jesus Christ personally. They *conversed* with him and were experiencing his love. Every testimony seemed to be about a living Lord who brought light, life and joy into people's lives. Even the prayers were about *light*—in stark contrast to my life, which had been stumbling along in self-imposed darkness.

I knew this was my time of crisis. I had asked for light, and God was giving it to me. How was I going to respond? I heard myself saying, *Yes, Lord, I do believe you are the light of the world . . . that you do not want me to walk in darkness . . . and that you want to give me the light of life.*

That night, in the victory circle, I could see those young people were onto life. They were into something worth living for. They knew Christ. They had found the answers to the questions I'd been asking.

Into the Light

I watched as each student gave his or her testimony, placed a little stick on the fire as a public promise—a symbol of commitment—and then sat down on the far side of the circle. I could tell that as the evening wore on, those who hadn't moved would become more and more isolated from the larger group.

So there I was, once again under the stars, and still feeling lost at sea. Yet I somehow knew the answer to my dilemma was close at hand. So what would I do—just sit there? I remembered my prayer for God's light on that stormy night in the South Pacific just one month before. Was I going to do something about my relationship with God tonight, or would I continue to play the game? I kept hearing a voice inside: *Munger, why don't you receive me and respond? Look, you say you've been in darkness and you want light. You say you want to know the meaning of life, but you've not really come to me, the Source of life itself. Why are you so fearful of me, as though I were going to take life away from you, when instead I've come to give you life everlasting? Stop running so hard to escape from me.*

I was afraid. What would my friends think? It would be so embarrassing. No one close to me, apart from family, was a convinced Christian. I knew I'd be ashamed to be known as an out-and-out believer. Yet it had suddenly all become so personal. It seemed as though Jesus himself was coming to me, holding out his nailed-pierced hands, saying, *I am your friend . . . the best friend you'll ever have.*

I was one of the last persons to step to the front of the circle that night. I suppose I got up because I was just ashamed to sit passively any longer. I remember that as I stood before those students, I said something about wanting to identify myself with Christ and turn my life around and learn to know God better.

Those words spoken out loud, publicly, opened my eyes and set me free to begin to know Christ. I had finally been introduced to the ultimate Friend for whom my heart had longed. I was still light-years away from a commitment, but even though I'd not yet understood Jesus to be Lord and Savior, I had trusted what I knew of him as God, my saving, loving Friend. We had finally met in a significant way. It wasn't a full-blown relationship, any more than one date is equivalent to a marriage. But it *was* the start of a growing friendship, the point at which I moved toward trusting Jesus as Savior, Lord and giver of true life.

That is why my heart is always tender toward those who come to God without the process of being broken by sin. There are many introductions to Christ. Usually, sooner or later, a breaking process is required. Eventually each of us must face the guilt and the wrongness in our life. But that's not always the first step! For me, that night in the victory circle was when I faced the light for the first time in my life. It was the first move, as the Chinese say, in a journey of a thousand steps.

That's also why, in sharing the gospel, I don't try to determine whether someone has been converted. I leave that to God and allow people to say for themselves where they stand. I learned early on to let the Holy Spirit bear witness. I would say in leading a person to Christ, "Can you from the heart thank God that he has now forgiven you?" You can usually tell from the way they pray whether it's authentic, but even so,

I don't respond by saying, "Now you're converted." It's a journey, and the person has taken a good step forward.

Even the disciples did not meet Jesus and become committed for life on the spot. When they heard John the Baptist call him "the Lamb of God," they wanted to know more. So they asked him, "Master, where are you staying?" And he invited them to come and see, to check him out, as it were. They followed him and got to know him. They then learned more about him. They heard him preach, watched him perform miracles. Then, for all we know, they went back to their fishing boats.

It was later that they had their moment of truth, when Jesus called for action. That's when Jesus said, "Let's go do it." He didn't say, "Men, think it over for a week or so, and let me know how you feel about my proposal. I'll come back in a few days and you can tell me if you want to go along with me or not." No! He simply said, "Follow me," and started walking. The disciples didn't worry about the risks involved, whether Jesus was a fake, who was going to run the family store. They simply listened to the Master and followed him.

But it's important to realize that there was a foundation in the disciples before Jesus asked for a serious commitment. When we ask people to make a commitment to Christ, whether it's the first step of faith or a challenge to a deeper level of obedience, that foundation of knowing something about Jesus is important. Following Jesus means fullness of life, not simply sacrifice for its own sake. I try to point to that life and let people come into it as far as they are ready.

The disciples didn't have much light at the moment of their decision, but they had enough light to take that first step. And that's all God requires of any of us when our needs intersect his ability to meet our need, when we find ourselves ready to be rescued from our own stormy seas by our Captain, personal Savior and Friend.

2
Commitment:
A Change
of Course

THE CHRISTIAN CAN BE VICTORIOUS

IN LIFE'S DIFFICULTIES BECAUSE HE CAN SEE

THEM AS TRANSITORY AND

ABSOLUTELY INCAPABLE OF SEPARATING

HIM FROM HIS HEAVENLY PURPOSE.

J. Lloyd Ogilvie, *God's Transforming Love*

The next lap of the journey took me from having an *acquaintance* with the Lord to the much more satisfying experience of *belonging* to him and letting him be my Captain, in charge of every part of my life.

True, I had finally discovered Christ as my Friend, and a friend was what I had wanted more than anything else in the world. I knew my life would never be the same from that day forward. For one thing, there would be some needed changes in my relationships because of this new friendship with the Savior, starting with my lifestyle at the UC-Berkeley campus. But that lifestyle was still firmly in my own control.

Because of my loyalty to my family and the moral standards I'd learned in that environment, I had chosen to abstain from liquor while in college. But one night during my senior year, I got drunk celebrating a Cal victory over the University of Southern California (USC). We were in a hotel in downtown Los Angeles, where our makeshift bar provided ample doses of orange juice mixed with straight alcohol. After only a couple of glasses of that noxious concoction, I was knocked flat. All my fraternity brothers had a good laugh, but it was no fun for me. I was never tempted to duplicate that experience.

Feeling All Alone

I could carry on with my brothers, have a good time and still keep my wits about me. The one thing I couldn't do was talk about my faith. My biggest fear was what my buddies would say about my experience with Christ. The term "Jesus freak" wouldn't become part of the Berkeley vocabulary until the radical sixties, but I knew my fraternity brothers would find their own epithet for me and my Christian experience. I was a sitting duck for verbal abuse and would surely be regarded as a weak-minded religious nut who needed a "Jesus crutch" to get himself through life. I was afraid and felt I would be left all alone.

Lost in my fears, I sometimes sensed the Lord speaking to me: *Munger, why do you distrust me? What's holding you back? You know who I am. I am the light of the world. You said you wanted to follow me. Well, I'm right here. But still you insist on sitting on your duff. If you don't make a move, how will you ever get into the light? You just don't understand, do you? Don't you know how much I love you? Now why don't you just come to me? I'll be waiting for you.*

Even though I knew I had a friend in Jesus, I still felt very much alone. I didn't know whom to talk to about my Christian walk. The carefully thought-out patterns of discipleship and training to be taught later by men like Dawson Trotman of the Navigators had not yet been developed. The only personal encouragement I had at this time was from my father, who believed that if I'd just read my Bible it would do its own work in my life. Dad had given me a copy of Weymouth's translation of the New Testament, and every time I read it I remembered how much

God's Word had meant to me at Mount Hermon the previous summer.

Pain and Depression

During my last year of school I wanted to read the Bible. I wanted to know more about Christ and the Christian life. I wanted to experience something of what I'd seen in the lives of the college students the summer before. But wanting isn't doing.

During that final year at Berkeley I was the quintessential silent believer. Not only was I afraid of being teased, but I wasn't sure enough of what had happened to me at Mount Hermon—in fact, I honestly didn't know if anything really *had* happened. I wasn't comfortable talking about my faith until the following summer, when I finally committed my life to Jesus Christ and made a 180-degree change in direction.

Two words best summarize my final year at Berkeley: *pain* and *depression*. The effects of the crash of 1929 were still being felt everywhere. Money was tight, and people were living on the edge financially and emotionally. Many had already slipped over the edge. Millions of Americans had lost their jobs, their savings and their homes.

The spectacular rise in prices on the stock market from 1924 to 1929 had borne little resemblance to actual economic conditions. The boom in the stock market and in real estate, along with the expansion of credit and high profits for a few industries, had concealed basic economic problems. Thus the U.S. stock market crash in October 1929, with its huge losses, was not the fundamental cause of the Great Depression. Still, the crash sparked and marked the beginning of the most traumatic period of modern American history.

During those unsettled times only the privileged few could afford to enjoy a fraternity or sorority experience. In fact, only the well-off could afford to send their sons and daughters to university at all. Thousands of students had to drop out of school to help put bread on the table for their families.

Always the "Honest Seeker"

As new house president of our fraternity, I had to worry about whether we'd be able to float the Berkeley chapter of the Sigma Phi fraternity through another year. Somehow we made it—I don't know how. But an even greater and more important struggle for me was the internal battle I was waging with my faith. How could I possibly integrate my new relationship with the Lord with the worldly lifestyle of the fraternity? Wouldn't I have to go public with Jesus one day? Could I be a quiet Christian forever? On the other hand, could I maybe blend just a little of my old way of life with a clever measure of the new? I knew the answer to that one: such an attempt at compromise would be as effective as trying to mix oil and water.

Fortunately, I still felt lingering effects of the Mount Hermon experience I'd enjoyed the summer before. That, along with faithful church attendance my senior year, kept me solidly in the category of "honest seeker." With each week's attendance at church I found I was becoming increasingly sensitive to the things of the Lord. Despite my choice to tell no one about Jesus, I knew I was alive in Christ. I could see, hear, feel and touch the truth. At the same time there was so much I didn't know.

In the past when I went to church, I would wonder, *Why are people singing these hymns? Why are they listening so attentively to what the pastor is saying?* Now I was beginning to understand. I was hungry. I wanted the food that was being set before me. God was giving me a new awareness of what life is all about.

I started going to a Christian student group called Calvin Club, but it didn't appeal much to me. I guess I was still feeling superior to the Christians who attended. Looking back, I realize that I could have learned so much had I just stepped into the arena, made a commitment and gotten involved with those earnest young Christians. But at least I had my Bible, and I continued to read it daily as I prayed for God's guidance.

Dentistry or Ministry?

Toward the end of my senior year, I began to think more seriously about my life vocation. My first choice would have been to become a medical doctor, but I knew I had neither the commitment nor the dedication for that. I preferred a profession that would allow me to play golf on Wednesday afternoons and knock off all day Saturday. I wanted to find a life's work that would make me comfortable without requiring that I make house calls.

The more I thought about my hoped-for lifestyle, the more I felt that dentistry would suit me perfectly. So I made dental school my objective.

I knew I'd need to get a summer job prior to starting my studies in dentistry. I remembered the good experiences at Mount Hermon the previous summer and figured I could make some good money while at the same time enriching my relationship with God. By this time much of the joy of knowing God the previous summer at Mount Hermon had departed, and I knew I needed to get back to the Lord to recapture the reality and freshness of my Christian faith. I applied for a job at Mount Hermon.

I was accepted as a member of the grounds crew. My tasks were things like sweeping out the auditorium after meetings, helping to make repairs on the many miles of scenic, redwood-lined trails, and cleaning the swimming pool. Fortunately for me it wasn't all work: whenever possible I would take in one of the many Bible classes that were offered.

One of my favorite Bible teachers was Dr. Francis Russell, who held forth every Sunday at 10:00 a.m. in an outdoor circle of redwood trees. One Sunday morning after cleaning the swimming pool I changed into a fresh shirt, put on a coat and tie, and walked the path from my tent to where Dr. Russell had just begun speaking. As I sat down, he announced as his text 1 Corinthians 15:58: "Be ye stedfast, unmoveable, always abounding in the work of the Lord, forasmuch as ye know that your labour is not in vain in the Lord" (KJV). He then drilled home two questions that landed in my fertile heart: "Are you living your life in the light of eternity? As Christians, you have a great future ahead of you. But are you aware that you will be asked to live the life of a servant?"

Crisis Time

Russell stopped me in my tracks. After all, Munger had big plans. I was going to become a dentist, join the cloistered privileged in an upscale country club, take Saturdays off and live a cushy life. What could that possibly have to do with my being a servant? I wanted to make money and, perhaps, love God on the side. Now Dr. Russell was forcing me to consider some alternatives.

But these insights hadn't really come upon me all at once. For many months I had been reflecting on the Bible and the new light it was shedding on my darkened life. In the end it was the Word of God that got to me, reminding me over and over not to spend my life "in vain." I was now ready to listen.

As an avid football fan I quickly drew on that sport for an analogy for what was going on in my life. I thought of the difference between the relative simplicity of a touch football game and the challenge of playing on a major collegiate or professional team—something that would take work and long-term commitment. I started asking myself what my work or service for Christ would look like one hundred years from now. I thought, *Maybe there really is more beyond what I know now.*

As Russell's message sent one dart after another into my awakened consciousness, I started to get the message that I would be stupid if I didn't live *now* for the eternal life that was yet to come. I slowly began to recognize that to continue to work toward a career in dentistry was not the most important thing I could do for myself or for the Lord.

I shared my questions and concerns with some friends on the staff, but most of them were younger and not in tune with where I was at the time. I had graduated and was ready to choose a vocation; they were still in process. I found myself literally in the woods, thinking, praying, worrying, talking to myself. I knew it was crisis time. I had to make up my mind.

One day I went to my tent, knelt by my bunk and prayed, *God, I've been trying to run this life all by myself. I still don't really know what you want done or how to fulfill what is best for me and for you. But as of this moment, I turn my life over and want you to take charge!*

Without knowing it, I was praying what I would eventually learn was question one of the Heidelberg Catechism: "What is your only comfort in life and in death?" The answer to that question is,

> That I, with body and soul, both in life and in death, am not my own, but belong to my faithful Savior Jesus Christ, who with his precious blood has fully satisfied for all my sins, and redeemed me from all the power of the devil; and so preserves me that without the will of my Father in heaven not a hair can fall from my head; yea, that all things must work together for my salvation. Wherefore, by his Holy Spirit, he also assures me of eternal life, and makes me heartily willing and ready henceforth to live for him.

I had finally done it! In truth I belonged to God. This time I knew my commitment was genuine. The summer before I had become personally acquainted with my Captain. I'd been willing to get to know him better, but until now I hadn't been ready to let him run my life. Now Christ was asking me to sign on as a member of the crew, come on board and launch out into the unknown.

Back in the fraternity, whenever I had prayed the Lord's Prayer, I had skidded around the phrase "Thy will be done on earth as it is in heaven." I didn't want that to happen, because I thought I knew more about what would be pleasant and fulfilling than God did.

The basic conversion experience happens, I think, when you acknowledge that you're no longer your own. I might have been a believer the summer before, but my life wasn't yet changed. Now I was taking the step of confessing Jesus as Lord.

Regardless of how we have come to Christ, the real process of spiritual formation, of becoming a disciple of Jesus, begins only as we allow him to be Lord. The Twelve were not asked to simply believe certain

things about Jesus; they were called to follow him. And in following
him, they found themselves in a kind of in-service training. From the
way he responded to situations and people they caught his attitudes as
well as his acts. They were being changed—a group of ordinary people
were becoming the extraordinary servants of God who would soon turn
the world upside down.

Good Advice

Part of signing on with the Captain was learning the basics of seamanship. The summer was ending, and I wanted to put my faith into action
quickly and find out how to pursue that training. After talking it over
with my father and mother, who were overjoyed, the next thing was to
schedule a time with Dr. Russell. After all, he had really become my
pastor that summer. He knew all about ministry, and I was confident he
would give me solid counsel on how to think about my future.

I made an appointment with him a couple of days later and told him
about my commitment to Christ. His wisdom came through as he listened to me talk. Some pastors would have jumped at the opportunity
to tell one their "boys" how to get started *tomorrow* in Christian ministry. Not Dr. Russell. He didn't encourage me to run off to seminary and
prepare to serve God by becoming a preacher. He wasn't even particularly excited. Instead he said, "Robert, you don't even know the Bible.
You need to get yourself grounded in the faith. Why don't you consider
attending Bible school for a year? Study God's Word. Get a better understanding of God's will for your life. Get involved in some kind of Christian service or ministry. Then, perhaps, you can go on to seminary later.
You'll be able to profit from your seminary experience so much more
with that kind of practical background."

Those were marvelous words. I've thought of them often as students
and others have come to me over the past sixty years, asking for guidance regarding their future ministry. We pastors too often massage our
own egos by playing God with the lives of those who come to us for

counsel. Many preachers seem to think there's only one set path of preparation for Christian service—usually the one they have traveled! How wrong that is.

I thanked Dr. Russell for giving me such a strong sense of direction. I then talked it over with my father, and he agreed that going to Bible school was a great thing for me to do. One or two pastors I spoke with, however, seemed to think I was heading down the wrong trail, as if a Bible school education was a step down for someone who had graduated from university. But finally, having requested counsel from a number of people, and having carefully weighed the pros and cons of going to Bible school, I made my own decision. I would attend the Moody Bible Institute in Chicago, Illinois.

No More Wining and Dining
It wouldn't be easy. I'd graduated from Cal, but I still had responsibilities the first week of the fall semester, for I was chair of the entertainment committee for the national convention of our fraternity in Berkeley. It would be my job to take fraternity brothers from around the country to San Francisco and host them for the better part of a week. There they'd be wined, dined and entertained in a manner I knew would not honor my new Captain.

Even as an active member of the fraternity I had generally shied away from this kind of lifestyle. Now, as a committed Christian, I knew it wasn't for me. How could I give any kind of a witness to Jesus Christ when I'd been at a big party the night before? I knew I couldn't do it. I had to resign. I called my fraternity brother Jim Hind, my closest friend and companion on the trip to Australia, and told him of my decision.

"What in the world has happened to you, Munger? I've got to see you! I'll come down tomorrow night. Promise me you won't talk to anyone until you've talked to me," Jim responded.

Jim did come by, and we talked for two hours. He didn't—perhaps couldn't—understand what had happened in my life. But he knew *some-*

thing had happened, and that it had been a deep, real decision. He said he knew it wouldn't do any good to try to change my mind, so he'd just go ahead and tell the other brothers what I'd decided. The next day I wrote a formal letter of resignation to the fraternity. I indicated I was heading to Chicago to go to school.

But I didn't want to just duck out, so I decided to meet my brothers face to face to tell them the real reason I was leaving. I was not looking forward to the encounter. I knew that to many of my brothers it would be hilarious beyond belief that a member of their esteemed, sophisticated fraternity at Cal Berkeley, of all places, would become a clergyman.

The day of reckoning finally came. I had prayed much about what I would say and how I would say it. My simple prayer was, *Lord, give me the nerve to do what I need to do.* I parked my car across the street from the house and began the long, agonizing walk to the door. One of the brothers saw me and ran to his room, where he grabbed his vest and put it on backward so that it looked like clergy vestments, high collar and all. Out he came, unsmiling, hands gently steepled, posing as the stereotypical pious clergyman. You could hear the hoots and hollers for blocks. The brothers were slapping their thighs in uproarious laughter at my expense.

When I saw what was happening, my first thought was, *Munger, you've done it now. This is going to be nothing but pure pain! In fact, it's going to be even worse than you thought.* Then, just as suddenly as that forbidding terror had come over me, God gave me a gift I've never forgotten: an immediate, total absence of fear, an assurance that I was right, that God was right, that I was with him and that he could handle it.

As I mounted the steps to shake hands with the brothers, I sensed that they were more uncertain around me than I was around them. I knew who I was and where I was going. I had Christ. They did not. I read into their laughter things like, "I sure hope Munger's not right, because we're all in trouble if he is."

Finally—Conviction!

That night at our chapter meeting, I had the opportunity as an alumnus to give a "word of wisdom." I took my time and told them about my struggle to find meaning in life. I reminded them of my experience at sea and explained how my awareness of God's love and light was becoming more real day by day. I told them I had finally found a Friend on whom I could rely. I then said that I felt a tremendous sense of rightness about what I was doing, and that I knew for certain God was real and would be with me each step of the way. I did not give much of the gospel, but I did point to Jesus as the living Savior.

During that brief witness—something I hadn't had the guts to do during the entire year before—I think my brothers understood that I was changing my direction with deep conviction and feeling. They had always been respectful of a guy who was willing to take a dive into an uncertain, unproven future. I'll always be grateful to them for taking me seriously.

I learned a great lesson that night as I stood before my brothers. It's this: the most effective preaching often does not come from the pulpit. The best witness for Christ usually comes when one is simply being authentic. It's when we share our hurts, our struggles, our hopes, our lack of faith, our dreams and our unique perspective—not as those who have arrived spiritually, but simply as ones who have chosen to follow the light the Savior has provided. And this kind of authentic living is a primary qualification, more important than technique, for a Christian leader.

I had come a long way in my search for the light, starting with that terrifying night in the South Pacific when I was almost lost at sea. I felt a bit like the disciples when Jesus got into the boat and told them to launch out into deep water. But with Christ at the helm of my life, I knew I would arrive at my many future destinations in complete safety.

Now all I had to do was pack for Chicago, board the train and get on with my life. After all, I now had a Friend, a constant companion and faithful guide. I believed I would never feel lonely again. But I had no way of anticipating how I would feel a few days later, watching the lights of Nob Hill and the Golden Gate fade into the distance as my train rushed on its way to the Windy City.

3
Basic
Training:
Learning the
Ropes

The trip from Berkeley to Chicago would take three days and two nights, and I was looking forward to it. But these many years later, I still remember my deep sadness as I waved goodby to my parents through the window as the train pulled slowly from the station. I kept asking myself, *Why couldn't Dad have at least embraced me when he said goodby?*

But Dad had never found it easy to express his emotions. Even though Albert Munger was active in many community organizations—he taught a class of high-school boys, served as an elder in the church and was a pillar in the local YMCA—it was hard for him to be a father to his sons. He was a lot like the statue Venus, a person without arms, much like the man I had already become. At many family Christmas celebrations, we'd be ready to give Dad his special gift and he would mysteriously disappear—vanish! It was always difficult for him to receive anything from us. I'm sure he was afraid he would trip over his emotions.

I didn't much like it, but I knew I was just like my father. Whether others regard it as a character flaw I don't know, but even today I find it difficult to take credit or accept any recognition for acts performed, sermons preached or counsel given. I enjoy the affirmation as it comes my way, but I don't know what to do with it. I got that from my father.

I knew Dad cared deeply about me and the career I was about to embark on. He was proud of his son and had always given me sound, thoughtful advice. He prayed for me constantly, and I was confident that he would continue to pray for me every day while I was at Moody. But knowing all that didn't make up for the loss of what I had always hoped would be a deep father-son relationship. These many decades later, I continue to feel a huge vacant space in my heart which he could have filled had he simply thrown his arms around me and said he loved me the day I boarded the Southern Pacific for Chicago.

If any person ever could have been designed to be the mirror opposite of my father, it was my mother. She was authoritative and forthright, particularly with us children. To disagree or argue with my mother was wrong, very wrong. Yet her love came through to me in the way she expressed concern about my health, my habits and my "being a good boy." She could be so intimidating that I wouldn't dare cross her. But she was always approachable and thoroughly human, whereas my father was aloof and distant. I hadn't thought much about my parents' influence on my life in recent days, but now that I was leaving on my voyage into the unknown, a heightened awareness of who they were and how they'd shaped my life flooded my consciousness.

God Speaks

I craned my neck to catch one final glance of my mother and father as they stood waving to me on the train platform. Then suddenly they were gone, lost in the darkness of so many farewells. The train rounded the Kern bend heading northeast, and I caught my last glimpse of San Francisco and the brilliant lights shimmering over the bay.

As everything around me went dark, a shroud blanketed my spirit. At once I felt totally alone. This was a venture even riskier and more daring than the trip to Australia had been. I was leaving my comfortable past to go to a place where I had neither friends nor family. Anxiety chilled my heart.

My mind raced: *Maybe I should have gone to dental school after all!* It's amazing how our minds fabricate an array of doubts, fears and suspicions when we start feeling sorry for ourselves. As I settled into my upper berth, the impact of my decision to go to Bible school swept over me like so many waves at sea. Why was I doing this? Was my mandate to go to Bible school really from the Lord? I didn't even know enough theology to make interesting conversation. When and how would I know if I'd made the right decision?

During those painful moments of lonesome reflection, the Lord again spoke to me. It wasn't an audible voice, yet I heard him say, *Munger, you really feel lonely right now, don't you? You're scared. You may even think you've made the wrong decision. I understand what you're feeling. There's just one thing I want you to know . . .* And then, from the wells of my memory—maybe the memory of a Bible class at Mount Hermon—I heard the Lord say, *Lo, I am with you always.*

Unbelievable! My Friend was once again making a commitment to me. He was saying, *I'm never going to leave you. I'll never forsake you. I'll always be at your side, no matter where you are, whatever your circumstances. You can count on me. So cheer up. You're not losing anything as long as I'm along.* I think what the Lord was really saying was, *Munger, grow up and quit crying like a baby!*

The awareness of his presence warmed me and then steadied me—not only on my trip to Chicago, but throughout the entire lonely eight months I would spend as a student at the Moody Bible Institute. I lived and breathed the promise that he would always be my faithful Captain and loyal Friend. I received strength and courage from knowing he had climbed on board my ship and would see me through the storms and uncharted waters of my life as a would-be student of the Bible.

The Depression Continues

Chicago was immense. The noise of the traffic, the roar of the elevated trains, the bustle of downtown and the huge buildings were more than I could take in. People seemed to be speaking every language and dialect known to humankind. They were all shapes, sizes and nationalities, rich, poor and middle-class, living among the ribbons of concrete, the brownstones, the wretched tenements of a huge metropolitan area—all in full view of a wet-behind-the-ears fraternity boy fresh from the posh comforts of a northern California suburb.

Futurist Alvin Toffler would not coin the phrase for decades, but I had already experienced what he would call "future shock," and I wasn't sure I liked it. For the first time in my life I saw poverty in the raw, exacerbated by the Great Depression, which had everyone teetering on the edge of financial and emotional survival. Banks were going on a moratorium, preventing people from withdrawing cash. As business failures increased and unemployment soared, yet people with dwindling incomes still were required to pay their creditors, it was apparent the entire nation had fallen into economic breakdown.

From 1930 to 1933, industrial stocks lost 80 percent of their value. In the four years from 1929 to 1932, approximately eleven thousand U.S. banks failed (44 percent of the banks that had existed in 1929), and about two billion dollars in deposits evaporated. The gross national product, which for years had grown at an annual rate of 3.5 percent, declined at a rate of over 10 percent annually, on average, from 1929 to 1932. Welcome to the Great Depression.

And welcome to Chicago! As if the economic news weren't bitter enough medicine, we worried about Al Capone and his notorious gangs, who were page-one news every morning. Capone and his hoodlums seemed to enjoy one field day after another on the violence-plagued streets of the Windy City.

But the Depression and the exploits of Al Capone notwithstanding, I had come to Chicago to study God's Word, and in the process to do my best to determine God's plan for my life. Dr. Russell at Mount Hermon had implied—correctly—that I didn't know Goliath from Gethsemane and that until I learned something about the Bible I wouldn't be much use to anyone as a purveyor of the gospel.

I had not realized that God would teach me as much about the suffering and sinfulness of human life as he would about salvation and the promise of life in Christ. For many of Chicago's poor, home was a sidewalk vent through which warm air would blow from large office buildings. This narrow blast of warmth was the only thing that kept some people from freezing in zero-or-lower temperatures.

One evening I was going back to my room at Moody, when an African-American man my age walked over to me from one of these sidewalk vents. He asked me for some money for food. As I gave it to him, I noticed that he seemed to want to engage in conversation. I don't remember giving him the gospel or even a word of Christian comfort, but I must have said something to catch his attention, because after we had chatted cordially for a few minutes, he asked me if I'd like to come to his apartment. He said it was only a few blocks away.

Rude Awakening

I'll never forget the impression his tenement house—almost next door to Moody Bible Institute—made on me. Everyone I saw as I entered that place of misery was poor, hungry, out of work and severely depressed. In total darkness, we groped our way to the third floor.

"Why are there no lights?" I asked.

"Light bulbs are expensive, so people steal them and use them in their own apartments. It's the only way they'll ever have any light," he answered.

Frightened, I stepped into his apartment, only to be met by the wizened faces of a half-dozen hungry, poorly clothed children lying lethargically about the room. My fear quickly turned to shame, anger and frustration. *Why didn't someone tell me about people like this? Why is*

my world so different from theirs? I didn't know what to say. I'm sure
I must have looked like a fool standing in front of them in my neatly
pressed suit, starched shirt and colorful tie. I wanted to say something
that made sense, but I didn't know the gospel, so I couldn't give them
the stirring words of the apostle Paul or the key points to the Sermon
on the Mount. I didn't even know the ABCs of Christian behavior, so
I could be of no help there either. All I knew was that good, conservative
Christians were to be morally clean and sexually straight and should not
drink, dance, smoke or chew.

I still marvel at my insensitivity to the people I'd been seeing every
day on the streets. It did not occur to me to seek some way to help meet
the desperate physical needs of those around me—and as I look back,
I realize that Moody Bible Institute as a whole was similarly insensitive.
I'm sure I dropped a few dollars in an outstretched hat now and then,
but I could have done much more during eight months in Chicago to
let the poorest of the poor know that I cared about their bodies as well
as their souls.

Without my knowing it, though, God was planting the seed of poverty
awareness in my spirit. I should probably be further along by now—I
am still trying to catch up with the stark reality of the injustice, discrimination and flagrant wrong that are being imposed on millions around
the world.

I had come to Moody to be mentored by a school, teachers and a
Christian perspective that I hoped would prepare me for a life of service
to One who had become my most intimate Friend. I did learn many
things at Moody, but I did not leave prepared to take on my own
responsibility for the social conditions I would encounter.

Spiritual Mentor
From its beginnings, Moody Bible Institute never placed much emphasis on academic degrees. Instead its mandate was to provide solid,
biblical, practical training in the Christian life and evangelism for those

who planned to enter secular fields of endeavor. Later, courses were added for pastors. At the time of my enrollment, Moody was regarded as the strongest and best school of its kind in the country. I often found myself giving thanks to God for Dr. Russell's wisdom in suggesting that I attend a Bible school. Sooner or later I *would* know the difference between Gethsemane and Goliath. When I did, Dr. Russell would be the first to know!

The entire environment of Moody became my spiritual mentor; its first president, James M. Gray, was the teacher who made the greatest impact on my life as a student there. In addition to his other formal responsibilities, Dr. Gray taught Synthetic Bible, giving an overview of the Scriptures. In his masterful teaching style he would point us to the entire sweep of the Bible day after day, allowing us to see up close the major themes of God's Word and the overall consensus of biblical truth. Once we had seen the large picture, he believed—rightly—we would be more competent to analyze and exegete the Bible in detail in other courses.

G. Campbell Morgan, another great Bible scholar of the day, said in his biography that he would often read a book of the Bible fifty times or more before beginning a detailed analysis of it. When asked why, he said that reading, rereading and rereading Scripture would help one see the basic truths in bold relief and gain a greater, fuller comprehension of the details.

Dr. Gray followed a method like Morgan's. Our first assignment was to read the first ten chapters of Genesis at least three times. He then had us memorize a five-word outline that he knew would serve us well for the rest of our lives.

It did. Four years later, when I was coming up for presbytery examinations—and I admit I was never a top student when it came to remembering facts and figures—I was able to do rather well on the English Bible portion of the test. When the examiner asked me how I knew so much about the Bible, I said, "Synthetic Bible study at Moody Bible

Institute, compliments of Dr. James M. Gray."

Here I need to share a deep concern. It's unfortunate that many students in our seminaries are not given a strong exposure to the basics of biblical understanding. Many students I have taught in seminary have come into my classes as biblical illiterates. Perhaps this is because many administrators and school benefactors feel seminary should be a sophisticated graduate school, delving into religious theory, rather than a place to learn and practice the practical. Perhaps we feel it is insulting to assume a student doesn't know the Bible. But let's be realistic. Most men and women who enter seminary do not know the Bible. Unless we drop our assumptions, we will continue to graduate "students of the Bible" who leave school as ignorant of biblical basics as they were when they entered. These students will know how to exegete, but they will not know how to *apply* salient biblical principles to themselves or to others.

I entered Moody as a special student. That meant I took elective courses as I desired, without working toward a specific degree. I just wanted to learn. I already had experienced a deep, personal friendship with my Captain, but I lacked the solid foundation of Scripture on which to build my Christian life. That's where Moody made the difference.

Learning the Basics

Among the many building blocks I gained during my eight months of study was the school's constant emphasis on God's gracious provision for our salvation, to be received only by trusting him and giving oneself over to him. Over the years this truth has remained the foundation stone by which I have evaluated the validity of whatever message or theology I am reading or studying. It has given me a fulcrum on which to stand: solid, sure and secure.

Whenever we are reading someone's theology, we need to ask ourselves: In this system of thinking, is Jesus Christ alive from the dead, offering himself freely for the sins of the world, or is he somewhere over in the margins, or perhaps not present at all? This is a key question. And when we hold to the centrality of Jesus Christ beyond question, we can field such questions with great assurance.

Another spiritual building block for me was to learn and believe in my heart that the Bible is God's Holy Scripture and the only infallible rule of faith in life. It was at Moody I learned that God's Word is the bread of life. We read in Matthew 4:4 that humankind cannot live by bread alone, but by every word that *is proceeding*—present tense, continual action—from the mouth of God. This means God not only quickens us through the word of the gospel but also *supports* us by the word of truth in Scripture. Simply put, if you and I are to sustain life, we must feed constantly on that Word. Conversely, if we fail to hear it, be nourished by it, appropriate it and live in it, we invariably will find ourselves spiritually undernourished, weak and unable to perform the tasks the Lord has placed before us.

Coach Vince Lombardi used to tell his players, "Fatigue makes cowards of us all." That's a good word for us as leaders teaching others how to play the game of life. Here and around the world there are millions of Christians who lack the courage, stamina and resolve to meet the enemy head-on simply because they don't have the energy—the spiritual nourishment of God's Word—to fight the battle! All this in spite of the hours in Sunday school, the countless sermons heard and family Bible readings at home. I recall hearing that in one exam given to students entering seminary, the majority could not name five apostles.

Another revolutionary building block for the development of my spiritual life was prayer. By now you may be thinking, *Munger, didn't you know how to do anything spiritual before you went to Moody?* I'm afraid I didn't. I didn't know the Bible, I was scared to death to witness to anyone, I hadn't memorized a single verse and I knew nothing about prayer.

Sure, I had said my "Now-I-lay-me's" as a child, and had intoned "Please help me, God!" more than a few times as I struggled to keep from being swept into the stormy Pacific, but I had no idea what real prayer is all about. That would soon change: I found out how much I didn't know about prayer my first week at Moody.

Learning to Pray

For my practical ministry I was assigned to join a group of eager young men who went regularly to Cook County Hospital to minister to the sick and the dying. Before we left for the hospital each week, our group of six to eight students would gather for a circle of prayer. I had never prayed out loud in my life. I couldn't even pray the Lord's Prayer. In fact, I had never even prayed over meals as a child, because that was my father's prerogative. For some unknown reason, the kitchen table in our home had remained the private pulpit of my father during my growing-up years.

Now here I was with my friends, with the inevitable about to happen. My palms were sweating and my heart raced wildly. We were kneeling in a circle, facing outward. Everyone in our group prayed fervently for the evening of hospital ministry to come. It was my turn. Embarrassed, I was frozen in silence. They waited and waited for me to say something, but there was no sound from Munger. Finally, mainly because the bus was about to leave, the leader concluded our prayer session, and we were on our way to the hospital.

Determined never to be embarrassed again, the next time our circle got together I was prepared with a handwritten note that I took out of my Bible and read while on my knees. It said, simply, "Dear God, help us in this experience." Perhaps it wasn't the most profound prayer ever to fall on the ears of the Almighty, but for me it was a refreshing start. It was my first prayer, the exciting beginning of a lifetime of disciplining myself to talk with God.

Since that time, I've always encouraged people who have difficulty praying to start by writing out their prayers and then reading them, whether in a group or in private devotions. That's because learning to pray is much like learning a foreign language. It may be difficult in the

BASIC TRAINING: LEARNING THE ROPES

first, seemingly futile attempts, but in time the one who prays will become open and free in expressing thoughts and feelings to the Father.

Five Stages of Prayer

Decades later, at Fuller Theological Seminary, each time I told that story of my first prayer I would hear a collective sigh of relief from large sections of the classroom. I realized that things hadn't changed much—students still didn't know how to pray. With that in mind, I spent many sessions with those young would-be ministers and missionaries going over the most rudimentary aspects of prayer. At Moody I learned to identify five basic stages of prayer, and at Fuller I shared these same stages year after year with my seminary scholars.

1. Prayer is *"Help me, Lord."* This is the "thrown overboard" stage, when we know we cannot make it on our own and must be rescued. We're struggling, clinging to the raft, hoping against hope that we'll be saved. Here we come to the place of saying simply, "Father, help me. I need you desperately, and I need you now."

2. Prayer is *a bigger, stronger hand clasping the hand of the one who prays.* When we pray this prayer, we soon discover there really is someone at the end of our outstretched hand. This is our first awareness, perhaps, that there is someone who can give us rest, who will intervene on our behalf, who will help us onto the life raft. We come to know with certainty that we can quit struggling for our own survival, because the firm hand of our Captain and Friend has rescued us.

3. Prayer is *a response to being rescued.* While often forgotten, this prayer is when we say "thank you" to God for plucking us from the stormy sea. It is resting in the arms of the One who never tires, who will always be there and who promises to stick closer to us than our dearest earthly friends.

4. Prayer is *interceding for our own deepest needs.* In this stage we are finally engaging in adult conversation with the Father. We are now in dialogue with the One who loved us enough to die for us, the one

who wants to say yes to our supplications.

5. Prayer is *reaching toward others in interpersonal intercession.* In this prayer we become the bridge between the hurting person and the Savior. We act—we *do* something. We reach out to another who's struggling to reach the raft. This godly compassion for the despair of others throws us into missions both at home and abroad. Suddenly we begin to feel the physical and spiritual pain of those around us and far away. We become sensitive to injustice wherever it arises, and we marshal every effort to see that right prevails where wrong has been king.

Expected to Be Missionaries

Learning to pray led me into yet another major building block in my spiritual growth—evangelism: sharing the good news, communicating the faith and leading people to a saving knowledge of Jesus Christ. As students we often heard how D. L. Moody would not go to bed at night until he had witnessed to someone about Christ. On more than one occasion he would get up after retiring, put his clothes on, go outside and find someone on the street with whom he could share the way of salvation. Only then would he go back to bed.

I admit I never arrived at that stage of spiritual commitment, but I was challenged nonetheless. Every time I'd get a haircut or ride a bus or streetcar, I sensed the importance of sharing my faith. I didn't always do a very good job of it, but from time to time I felt the Lord did enable me to be a faithful witness for him.

Here again, much of our seminary teaching today falls terribly short. We need to put aside our sophistication, take a page from the Bible school handbook and come back to evangelism. Most students in seminary—liberal and conservative schools alike—simply do not learn what the Christian life is all about. Jesus is not theory. He is not thick books on esoteric subjects. Unquestionably the ability to exegete difficult passages of Scripture can be valuable for preaching. Knowing biblical facts and laboring over the grammar of the original tongues can make for powerful sermons, but these are *not* the key issues of our faith. It's vital that we discipline ourselves to know what God's Word says and then be willing to share with others that good news of Jesus Christ.

I didn't know it when I enrolled, but I soon learned that at Moody we were expected to be missionaries. It was not an option. I suppose I still see myself as a frustrated missionary. I wanted to serve overseas, but for health reasons I never could. At least I have the comfort of knowing I volunteered for service, giving God a chance to give me the thumbs up if he so desired. He didn't!

God never opened the doors for me to engage in service abroad, but he has done nothing but open doors here at home and around the world during my many subsequent years of ministry as *player-coach*— Elton Trueblood's great word for the Christian leader who is involved with a great team in the big game of life.

A Reluctant Witness

At Moody I was constantly being exposed to prayer meetings, was given opportunities for evangelism and took part in Bible studies, missionary prayer bands and chapel services—all of which were foundational material to nurture my spiritual development, and all of which have remained a great part of my life. I was being mentored.

But I remained a reluctant witness. We were required to keep careful records of what we did in our practical work of evangelism, whom we talked to, decisions made and so on. This was embarrassing for me— my reports were never anything to write home about. Week after week my report read 0, 0, 0, 0, 0. This was big-time discouragement for me.

I remember going up and down the elevator that first night at the hospital—the same night I was so embarrassed that I didn't know how to pray out loud. This was high drama for me. I refused to get out of the elevator on my appointed floor, because I knew I would fail again. I'd pass my floor, go to the top floor, travel down to the lobby and then come back up again, without ever leaving the elevator. I could not muster the courage to get off the elevator. What was the point? No one would get saved. No life would be renewed or changed. No one had yet rededicated his life to Christ because of my witness.

My friends kept trying to encourage me by saying, "Munger, just give them the gospel." That was probably great advice. The only problem was that I didn't know the gospel—definitely not a plus when one is trying to share the good news.

Each week I would go to Cook County Hospital to minister to the sick and would return to Moody with no successes to report. Entering the men's ward, I'd start a spirited conversation with someone about the weather, politics, sports or his health, and then I'd leave as quickly as I'd come. It was no more than a casual visit, hardly what D. L. Moody had in mind when he painstakingly instituted his basic course in practical evangelism. It was his idea for us to go out and make disciples, not social calls.

One night, in that hospital elevator, again traveling up and down in fear and trepidation, I prayed, "Lord, you've got to get involved here. If I can't do a simple assignment like this, I'm going to be an abysmal failure in any kind of future ministry. If you don't help me, then why should I stay in this school, and why should I go into the ministry?" I meant it. I needed a miracle fast.

During that final, desperate prayer, God spoke to me as clearly as he had on the train the day I left Berkeley for Chicago. He said, *I'll be with you. I've heard your prayer.*

And he did. From that moment on, I simply turned my life and witness over to the Father. I quit trying to do things in my own strength. I started listening to the men in the hospital ward. I found I could meet them at their point of loneliness—and they were all lonely. I discovered that giving a sick man just half an hour of my time was like giving him a bag of gold. So many had no one who cared whether they lived or died. I would just ask them how they felt and what their concerns were.

One twenty-six-year-old man afflicted with syphilis told me what a mess he'd made of his life. I asked him if God had any place in his life at all. "No," he said, "I know there's a God around somewhere, but I don't feel I ever have any touch with him."

I had finally memorized John 3:16—the extent of my Bible memorization thus far—so I shared the passage with him. I then told him what faith meant, that it was simply trusting someone else to do something very important for you, something you could not do for yourself. I was talking from my heart. I was simply talking about my Captain and Friend, Jesus Christ.

Our Supreme Joy

Finally, in a cold sweat, I blurted out, "Joe, would you like to receive Christ as your Savior?"

You could have knocked me down with a feather when he said, "Yes, I would. I would like to know I am forgiven."

That moment was the turning point in my Christian experience. Ever since that memorable day more than sixty years ago, I've reminded thousands of students and members of my various congregations that once you see a person being born again and coming to faith in Jesus Christ, it spoils you for anything less in Christian ministry.

As Christian leaders we will be doing many different things to see that the kingdom of God is advanced. But the supreme purpose and joy of our calling will always be to see people born again, joining the forever family of God with a personal knowledge of Jesus Christ.

Grasping the truths of the Bible, learning to pray and to share my faith—these were my key areas of growth during my time at Moody Bible Institute. They proved to be the fundamentals of seamanship as I began to navigate with my Captain. I was becoming a disciple, following Jesus and finding myself involved with people and events that took on eternal significance. In a way I was experiencing what the disciples experienced following Jesus: seeing him minister, teach and heal and being given the chance to try it out themselves. Jesus didn't set up a school for training religious professionals; he called together a group of ordinary men and trained them to do exactly the things that he was doing.

The church is still most effective where laypeople are equipped and encouraged to do the work of ministry. As a pastor I've seen the exciting results of imparting those basic skills of Bible study, prayer and witnessing that I received from my mentors and fellow students at Moody.

Now I was ready to take the first steps of leading others into discipleship. This first "officer's training" occurred during my formal theological education at Princeton Theological Seminary, the next port of entry for a young man continuing on an exciting voyage of discovery with his faithful Captain and Friend.

4

Advanced
Training:
Lessons
in Navigation

A CHRISTIAN MAN IS THE MOST

FREE LORD OF ALL,

AND SUBJECT TO NONE;

A CHRISTIAN MAN IS THE MOST

DUTIFUL SERVANT OF ALL,

AND SUBJECT TO EVERYONE.

Martin Luther

The late great football coach Vince Lombardi was a devout churchman and dedicated family man. He was also a person of honesty and integrity who was a fanatic for excellence, mercilessly demanding 100 percent effort at a time when such virtues were being not only largely ignored but even ridiculed. Those values appear page after page in a book Lombardi wrote about his relationship with football, the game he loved. In *Run to Daylight* Lombardi gives us a how-to series of "lessons for life" that make sense whether football is of serious interest to the reader or not. One particularly apropos lesson appears in his chapter on running backs.

Run to Daylight

Lombardi describes how football players learn their plays and then practice them until they become as automatic as breathing. During a game, then, the players can instinctively pull from their memory banks the numbers, the signals, the advice and the hours of coaching. But as the running back gets the ball, tucks it under his arm and begins his rush down the field, he has time to consciously remember only one thing: he must *run to daylight!*

When I read Lombardi's chapter for the first time, I knew I was never going to be a confident running back, eagerly taking the ball toward the end zone. I was often reluctant even to get my hands on the ball.

Most of the time I felt more as if I was being led by my Father with a lantern. The darkness was scary, but as long as he led me I felt secure. But Lombardi's image of daylight appealed to me, because I knew that my Captain himself was the light. I knew God was telling me to keep walking in the light. He was saying, *Munger, you know light when you see it. I've taught you some plays, and you've been pretty good at being disciplined. Now I want you look for those shafts of light I'm putting before you day after day. Your primary task now and for the rest of your life and ministry is to walk in my light.*

I had lived in darkness long enough and had longed for a true friend. Now I had found the light and that Friend, one who promised he would stick closer to me than a brother. Again and again over the years I have been deeply moved by the story of Jesus healing the blind man as recorded in John 9. There Jesus not only is the bringer of light, he is himself the light. I am the light of the world, Jesus said; if you come to me, if you follow me, if you run to this light, you will have life.

As I left the Moody Bible Institute and, after another brief summer interlude in California, headed for Princeton Theological Seminary and the continuation of my theological studies, I knew I was walking toward daylight. The dark clouds of confusion and doubt had lifted. My spirits were beginning to soar. I was still only a member of the crew and desperately needed to learn the ropes of spiritual navigation. But regardless of whether I would accomplish my life goals, I was confident God would always be at my side, illuminating my path. I needed only to stay focused on his light, even though at times I felt frustrated, perplexed and anxious about my future.

Theologically Extreme?

It was the fall of 1933, the beginning of my first year at Princeton Seminary in New Jersey. The day I checked in I learned that two of my Mount Hermon friends, Dave Cowie and Clyde Kennedy, had registered the same day. What a coincidence, I thought. Or was it God's hand reuniting us "California crazies"? I know now it was the latter. It wasn't long before we had rekindled our friendship and determined together to take on the world.

Several who were studying with us at Princeton soon came to regard us as theologically extreme. Students and faculty members alike saw us as zealots who might just as well have arrived from a distant planet. Looking back I can see why.

Our California contingent was joined by a few from Wheaton College, then by others. After we had sampled all the local church fare and found it less than to our liking, we decided to start a fellowship of our own. We were confident that this new, improved *koinōnia* experience would be relevant and exciting for all who got involved with us. How could it not meet the spiritual needs of those students who were being so shortchanged, we thought, in the relatively traditional ecclesiastical setting of Princeton and its environs?

Early in the fall our fellowship convened at the seminary's historic Alexander Hall, a magnificent early-nineteenth-century structure, architecturally symbolic of past glories and tradition. About fifteen students came that first night. We sang a few choruses and gave a word of witness, after which Samuel Zwemer, a great missionary to Arabia and Egypt, took over and unfolded to us a powerful, soul-satisfying exposition on prayer.

That evening was the beginning of something extraordinary for all of us, a fellowship that would keep us spiritually warm to the things of God. But like so much of what we would experience in seminary, we were unaware of how God would play the role of the relentless "hound of heaven" in leading, guiding and pushing us in areas of our deep desires.

We kept holding our Sunday-evening meetings until the Christmas holidays. All of this was bewildering to some of our colleagues. Many, by their attitude toward us, seemed to be saying, "What's going on with you? Trying to be supersaints? Can't you get enough of God and the Bible during class, chapel and Sunday-morning worship?"

Determined Witnesses

We weren't trying to be spiritual superstars, but down deep we were hungry for more of God. That's why our weekly fellowship was so vital. It provided the spiritual food, warmth and encouragement we were sorely missing; it was a weekly discovery that seemed to be the answer to the insatiable needs of our young, maturing minds. We knew that Jesus was the way, the truth and the life, and we were determined to share his love and truth in as direct a way as possible—even if we would have to endure being regarded as "the weird ones from the Wild West."

None of the criticism slowed us down. We were convinced that Jesus was at the door of people's hearts and would bring abundant life to whoever let him in. So it became our single-minded desire, even as young, inexperienced seminarians, to stand by that door, eagerly, passionately helping all who were looking for life-changing answers to find them in Jesus Christ.

Years later I would discover that the great Anglican preacher, communicator and theologian Samuel Moore Shoemaker had written a poem which spoke to what we were attempting to do during our fledgling attempts at witness at Princeton. Perhaps Shoemaker's verse will help you sense that same evangelical zeal we felt and encourage you to take your own position by the door.

I Stand by the Door

I stand by the door.
I neither go too far in, nor stay too far out.
The door is the most important door in the world—
It is the door through which men walk when they find God.
There's no use my going way inside, and staying there,
When so many are still outside and they, as much as I, crave to
    know where the door is.
And all that so many ever find
Is only the wall where a door ought to be.
They creep along the wall like blind men,
With outstretched, groping hands.
Feeling for a door, knowing there must be a door,
Yet they never find it.
So I stand by the door.
Go in, great saints, go all the way in—
Go way down into the cavernous cellars,
And way up into the spacious attics—
It is a vast, roomy house, this house where God is.
Go into the deepest of hidden casements,
Of withdrawal, of silence, of sainthood.
Some must inhabit those inner rooms,
And know the depths and heights of God,
And call outside to the rest of us how wonderful it is.
Sometimes I take a deeper look in,
Sometimes venture in a little farther;
But my place seems closer to the opening—
So I stand by the door.

Suffering Children

During the fall of my first year of study at Princeton, several members

of our group learned about a ministry opportunity in Trenton. Dave
Cowie, Clyde Kennedy, Bob Pierce, Otto DeCamp and I, along with a
few others, had no idea what to expect, but we had a message from the
Lord and we were ready. We had the confidence that if our small band
of servants used its gifts for the glory of God, we'd be prepared for
anything that might come our way.

What we were *not* prepared for was the terrible poverty and hope-
lessness we would discover in that decaying area that must have ranked
near the bottom in every social category. In the midst of the Great
Depression, hunger, despair and homelessness in North Trenton (just
a few miles south of the seminary) were wrecking individuals and de-
stroying the lives of thousands of families. Those hit hardest were children.

In Trenton we began to hear stories we'd never heard before—of
children who had never owned a toothbrush; children with no shoes
or socks and no warm clothing in subzero weather; scarce food; no heat
in the walk-up tenements; unemployment rising and expectations falling. Most of the children had to share the only bit of clothing they had—
a shirt, a blouse, a pair of shoes, a dress, a pair of trousers—with their
brothers and sisters. The youngsters were forced to go to school on
alternate days because there wasn't enough clothing to go around.

The depth of the poverty we saw ripped at our hearts. But even worse,
these children knew nothing about a loving heavenly Father. So we
started a mission Sunday school—for their spiritual well-being *and* to
help get them out of the cold.

Each Sunday it was my responsibility to teach the ninth-graders, a
tough group of youngsters to relate to because their attention span was
about as long as it takes to hurt if you step on a rake. I quickly learned,
though, that if I told them stories that communicated gospel truths in
ways they could understand, I could get them to track with me. In this
class I discovered a special love for teaching. I found I knew how to
share biblical truths simply. Before long I had developed a growing

confidence as a teacher, although I had my moments of both fear and surprise at the response I was receiving from the youngsters. I found myself embarking on an entrepreneurial act of faith that elicited enthusiastic participation from the kids. I was having a terrific time.

I realized that I was a visionary. I could see the end results of events that were still only shadowy, formative images in my mind. Like Lombardi's running back, I was off and moving toward the light.

Some might have seen our group as a team at the time, but we really had not yet come together as a cohesive force. Each of us had his particular niche, and we would come and go, ministering to the children according to our individual gifts. Still, as I look back at those years, it is now clear that what I would later call *teaming* in the truest sense of the word had its simple beginning at that Sunday school in Trenton.

The Beginning of the Teams

Every member of our group had a vital, unique gift, and each individual was encouraged to nurture and use that gift for ministry. Before long, my own spiritual outreach extended well beyond the mission Sunday school. But that experience with the children in beleaguered North Trenton provided me with the training I would soon use to lead others in effective team ministries.

In the spring of my freshman year at Princeton, a graduating senior asked me if I would take over the responsibility for recruiting and leading deputation teams—actually gospel teams—for the school. I said yes, knowing this would be an opportunity to gain valuable experience. My affirmative reply ultimately led me into one of the most important areas of spiritual development during my time at Princeton. Word quickly spread on campus of the earnest young seminarians who were spending their weekends talking about the Lord wherever they could capture an audience. I remember that the president of the seminary was less than enthusiastic about the nature of our team's work. He called us a group of "red-hot gospelers." A marvelous compliment, we thought.

Our group had rules, and participants were required to adhere to certain disciplines. One of these was attending a Friday-afternoon meeting for prayer and briefing. Another requirement—one I had learned at Moody Bible Institute—was that members of our gospel teams had to turn in reports each week, stating in writing where we had gone, to whom we'd spoken, what kind of group we talked to, how many decisions or rededications were made and so on. I learned one thing during this time: if you ask people to put down on paper what *really* happened in their meetings, they really go after it!

Enough students were attracted to this challenge and accountability that the team continued to grow. By the second year sixty students were involved. At the end of two years, even the seminary president publicly reported on the number of churches in which the gospel teams had ministered. (We felt this acknowledgment was a major coup!)

I'm convinced that I learned more about *ministry* (not about the Bible or theology) in the two years on the gospel team than in all my seminary study. This was the practical, workable stuff. In my formal classroom training, my mind was being stretched intellectually—something I needed and appreciated. I was given technical principles on how to navigate through complex theological waters. I learned the art of preaching and how to project my voice, and I reveled in the seminary's library with the vast reservoir of learning it was putting before me. Seminary was my guide, an inexhaustible supply of wisdom for my spiritual voyage.

The Art of Spiritual Leadership

At Moody Bible Institute I had operated out of the basic primer on seamanship. There I was a deck hand wanting desperately to be an officer. I longed to be trusted with leadership of some great endeavor under my Captain in the greatest of all causes. At Moody I learned the basics, the fundamentals of the art of spiritual navigation.

If Moody was my introductory course to seamanship, Princeton became my Annapolis. I was now in an environment where I could learn the basics of the art of spiritual leadership. I was becoming acquainted with the tools of my trade and was being taught how to use them. How grateful I am for the solid, evangelical training, so rooted in the authority of Scripture and sound Reformed theology, that Princeton gave me during those years.

But it was the weekend gospel teams that allowed me to put my theoretical navigational skills to the test. Our gospel teams ministered in churches, to youth groups and later to far-flung Civilian Conservation Corps (CCC) camps—places where hundreds of young people were so bored with what they were or weren't doing that they'd listen to anyone. We discovered, with joy, that we didn't even have to be experienced. Sometimes all we had to do was show up and be genuine.

Six Spiritual Lessons
Week after week the teams gave me a rich opportunity to put into practice everything I was learning in the classroom. Six specific spiritual lessons emerged from that team experience.

1. It was a powerful vehicle for much-needed *personal renewal.* The gospel team shook us up as individuals. It made a life-changing difference in every area of our lives—an impact that continues to this day.

2. We saw before us the power of a *personal witness.* This was not a new revelation for us. But because it was all so practical and hands-on, we realized that Christ actually wanted to use us to share his light with others. We saw that people, empowered by his Spirit, responded to the gospel. We learned that when we walked in his light, that light would keep moving us into one new area of ministry after another.

3. We discovered the power of a *cooperative endeavor.* We did things together. We shared our lives. Alone, I never would have had the courage to do what we did. But with the team at my side, I knew I would never be alone. The affirmation of the team made all the difference.

4. We felt the power of *in-service training.* Jesus was our model for

ministry. We observed that the Master (a) by instruction showed his disciples how to do ministry, (b) by example modeled it—lived it out, (c) by experience (clinical) had the disciples do it, (d) by holding them accountable saw them do it and (e) by affirming them watched them grow in wisdom, understanding and effectiveness.

5. We experienced the power of *encouragement and affirmation.* When one was down, another team member could lift that person up, help renew his confidence and encourage him to know that the team was with him all the way.

6. We learned the enormous power of *prayer.* We knew we couldn't do our ministry alone. Ours was a venturing faith that recognized we were nothing unless we spent time on our knees before the Lord.

I asked myself the question then, and I ask it today: What keeps the heart beating? Sitting around contemplating noble thoughts? Sitting at a desk? Watching fitness videos on television? Of course not. If you want a healthy heart you have to exercise, move around, get interested in something that demands a hefty supply of oxygen and adrenaline. If I had not been involved in the exercise of the gospel team, I wonder if I ever would have had the least notion of what spiritual adrenaline was all about.

A whole *is* greater than the sum of its parts. We learned early on that our team was effective only when it worked together. We loved each other and looked after each other. No one was allowed to critique the performance of another member until the following week. We risked together. We were winners even when we failed. We trusted each other and relied on each other. Week after week we demonstrated to one another God's love and forgiveness in practical terms.

Years later, in my ministry in South Hollywood, Berkeley, Seattle, Menlo Park, California, and finally Fuller Seminary, this concept of intimate teaming with the laity would become the core of my ministry. And God put it all in motion at Princeton Seminary when a small band of zealous seminarians who didn't know much about anything determined to make Christ known to any and all who would listen.

"We All Win"

Princeton was my trial run as a leader. It was my officer's candidate school where I learned to work with my fellow officers—the team. I spent my time acquainting myself with lifeboat drills, crew training, the compass, the maps, the sextant and the basics of the ship's maneuvers. But I was still docked in quiet waters close to shore, not yet put out to the rigors of the sea. That would come soon enough, in my first stormy assignment as a pastor in South Hollywood. For the time being I would remain busy attempting to master the basic science of spiritual navigation and taking advantage of the rich opportunity of coordinating the leadership of our teams.

If you have been—or are now—a part of such a ministry team, you understand what I'm saying. Because when we serve the Lord together in the unity of his love, nobody gets left out. We all win. This story that I recently found tucked deep in one of my files makes the principle clear:

A beautiful young girl whom the world would call retarded was getting ready to run at the Special Olympics. The gun went off, and she let out a yell, "I'm gone!" Now, this is not an Olympic-form runner. She's hitting every lane. But she has everybody beat by 40 yards. She got all the way down to the finish line and stopped—she would not go across. She turned and waited for her friends. And then, as all six young people held hands, crossing the finish line together, she said: "WE ALL WIN!"

That is the love of Jesus in action. That is the team at work. There is no playing to the gallery. It is only a nonaggressive, non-ego-centered spirit of love and cooperation that will give us true success in ministry. Here's the exciting part: the team, eventually, will make winners out of everyone—even if one loses.

On a team—whether it's the rough-and-tumble of the NFL or NBA, the fierce competition of a corporation, the uncertainties of living in a family, or the challenges of a pastor and his or her staff—individualism is out of place. Forget the screaming, cheering fans in the stands. Quit looking for personal glory. There's no place for it. If it is pursued, it will be fatal. Looking out for number one doesn't cut it. A deep love for the Lord Jesus Christ, a mutual dependence on the team and a commitment to honest, no-holds-barred, long-term accountability are vital for spiritual growth and will help prevent irresponsible personal behavior. And whether you are a "special Olympian," homemaker, disadvantaged child, pastor, factory worker, student, doctor, teacher or whatever, the spirit of the team will also work for you.

Jesus and His Team

One thing we still have to get through our heads: *no one needs a theological degree to be effective in ministry.* We need to be amazed once again at how Jesus trusted nonprofessionals with major responsibilities. I may have heard someone say that during my three years of academic study at Princeton, but I think I really learned it on the team. And the principles of teaming are as effective today as they were in Galilee two thousand years ago.

Jesus taught his disciples to work as a team. Their willingness to follow him, learn from him and work in unity with him and each other was all that was required. Why were they willing to do this? Because they knew the Master trusted them and would always be there to teach them.

Jesus traveled with his small band of men. He took time to answer their most banal questions. He didn't choose them because of their pedigrees—they had none, except perhaps the clout of a certain tax collector, and even his qualifications would later be subject to question. Instead Jesus took a ragtag contingent of uneducated, sweaty fishermen from their boats and nets and made them fishers of people. He dared to believe that ordinary people could become extraordinary servants of God. From a common lot of questionable personalities, he would call his disciples, whom in turn he would send out to disciple the nations. Today one of the single greatest bottlenecks to the spiritual renewal and outreach of the church continues to be the unscriptural division of roles between clergy and laity. Many clergy are hesitant to trust the laity with significant responsibilities, while laypeople are equally hesitant to trust themselves as ministers of Christ. Romans 12:3-6 in the Living Bible paraphrase sums up the truth of the matter as well as it can be said:

As God's messenger I give each of you God's warning: Be honest in your estimate of yourselves, measuring your value by how much faith God has given you. Just as there are many parts to our bodies, so it is with Christ's body. We are all parts of it, and it takes every one of us to make it complete, for we each have different work to do. So we belong to each other, and each needs all the others.

God has given each of us the ability to do certain things well. So if God has given you the ability to prophesy, then prophesy whenever you can—as often as your faith is strong enough to receive a message from God.

Teach One to Teach One

Not only did Jesus trust his team, but he took pains to teach them. Day after day Christ gave special attention to his small band so they might understand his message.

The setting of the Sermon on the Mount in Matthew 5:1 is significant: "Jesus saw the crowds and went up a hill, where he sat down. His disciples gathered around him, and he began to teach them" (TEV). This is a strange sequence indeed, and certainly not one followed by many of today's pastors, spiritual teachers or evangelists. Here's the scene: Jesus sees a vast multitude of people eagerly waiting to hear his words, and he turns on his heel, walks away and gathers his disciples around him for some impromptu teaching at the top of a nearby hill. Wasn't it rude to respond this way to the waiting throngs? Some had surely come from many miles away to see and hear the Master. Didn't

Jesus know this social miscue would be terrible public relations for him as an itinerant preacher claiming to be the Messiah, one who already had his share of negative ecclesiastical press?

But Jesus knew something we still struggle to understand. He knew the way to reach the multitudes was to teach others who in turn would share with others the Word of life. No ego was involved. PR was never an issue. Jesus simply made a commitment—and lived up to it—to take the time and energy to share truth with his leaders.

Later, Paul would write to his "son in the faith" in 2 Timothy 2:2, "Take the words that you heard me preach in the presence of many witnesses, and give them into the keeping of men you can trust, men who will be able to teach others also" (TEV). The apostle Paul caught it! He knew that if the church continued to follow the leadership principles initiated by Jesus, the truth of God's Word would be extended outward without limitation by teachers who were teaching others how to teach.

Today the high levels of theological awareness and advanced education of many lay men and women, along with the increasingly accepted and accelerated diversity and mobility of our society, are challenging the church. We need to break out of its traditional straitjacket of limiting the ministry to the domain of the pastor-teacher and to take seriously the nurture and development of a gifted laity that works together as a team for a more diversified and effective teaching ministry.

Making Time to Train

But trusting and teaching were only part of the disciples' growing, intimate relationship with the Master. Jesus took personal time to train his team, and his time-intensive methods of instruction have never been surpassed. His program included taking the time for explicit teachings in procedure and making the time to give his disciples practical, clinical experience.

Today if the church of Jesus Christ is to accelerate its outreach to the lost, those in spiritual authority have no choice but to make time and then *use that time* to teach, train and provide the modeling that is essential to any effective ministry. This will require more than a laity-oriented twenty-minute sermon a couple of times a year. This takes *real* time—quality time—and an unwavering commitment to training those nonprofessionals who have made the decision to serve their Lord and Savior whether the local pastor approves of it or not!

Christian leadership today must reflect the boldness we see in Jesus' relationship with his disciples. Jesus said, "Follow me," and they followed. They learned by observation. Jesus walked his disciples through one exercise after another. This took time, personal time. The long, painful hours, the boat trips, the walks along dusty Galilean paths, all combined with the boundless love and energy that Jesus poured into his team to make the difference.

Jesus didn't ask his disciples to take notes while he taught theory from the lofty lectern of a synagogue. He was down-to-earth and practical. Together they walked the roads, faced the crowds. They moved among the sick, the lame and the dying together. They slept side by side. They did cleanup jobs together.

The team enjoyed Jesus as a companion. They experienced the wonder of his daily presence. Jesus proved that time and love are a powerful combination. Without this combination of time and love in our ministries and in our lives, we will falter, struggle and ultimately fail.

Ministry is not a go-it-alone arrangement. It's a team effort or it's nothing at all.

The Master's Method

At Princeton I was fortunate enough to catch a brief glimpse of how Jesus mentored his team of disciples, and those insights were as valuable as all the formal training I received in ancient Bible languages, church history, homiletics and speech. Perhaps the following progression of how to teach others will also be your key to multiplying yourself and thereby enhancing the spiritual gifts of those who look to you for leadership and guidance. The sequence goes like this:

I do it—you watch (to learn)

I do it—you help

You do it—I help if necessary

You do it—I watch (to evaluate)

You do it—another watches you (to learn)

The process then continues, each one teaching one, until the fellowship is filled with men and women who, like so many accomplished deck hands, have learned the ropes and are ready to move out into spiritual navigation, instructing others. The point of it all is to be an effective witness for Jesus Christ and to share his message of life and hope with others.

In even a cursory look at the Gospels, one key strategy of the Master stands out: Jesus was acutely aware of the need to provide practical, clinical experience for his team. None of us would want to have surgery under a doctor who had managed to get an A in a course on *Gray's Anatomy* but had never scrubbed up or held a scalpel before. Most of today's medical schools place their students in the wards almost as soon as they enter the program. They need to begin their practical, on-the-job training immediately.

Perhaps it was risky for Jesus to trust his message and ministry of the kingdom of God to eager nonprofessionals who made one mistake after another. Still, Jesus did it, and the result of his time-intensive training was that his disciples returned shouting with joy (Lk 10:17). The venture of preaching and teaching in his name had demonstrated to them the delivering power of God. They discovered a confidence in Christ and in themselves they had not known before.

Four Questions

In light of Jesus' leadership strategies, help me answer these questions—I'm sure you will think of many more:

☐ Why do so many church leaders today shy away from the approach Jesus used to disciple the disciples? What are today's leaders afraid of? Why are so many unwilling to lift off their roofs and tear down their personal walls? Why are so few willing to take the time to do it right?

☐ Is there a better, more effective method to disciple today's laity than the modeling Jesus gave us to train the Twelve? If so, perhaps we'd better take the seminar. If not, what factors are holding us back from doing it right?

☐ Are the laypeople—the amateurs—really the vital link to keeping the ministry of the body alive, vibrant and growing? Or are we kidding ourselves in suggesting that leaders should "lead from below"? Again, what is keeping us from doing it right?

☐ Max DePree, author of an excellent book on leadership entitled *Leadership Jazz*, asks, "What can a leader learn by walking in the shoes of a follower?" And, I add, when our results are so poor, when pastors burn out, when accountability for our leaders is at an all-time low, what is keeping us from doing it right?

You'll recall that when the members of the Jerusalem council saw the boldness of Peter and John and recognized that these men were ordinary, uneducated nonprofessionals, they were amazed and realized what being with Jesus had done for them! The leaders of the Sanhedrin also were astounded, shaken to their sandals by the undeniable fact that the hopelessly crippled man whom they had seen day after day begging alms in front of the Gate Beautiful had been miraculously healed. They could not deny it. There he was—standing, walking, leaping in joy! This was discipleship at work, results produced by the Master who had poured his life into a few good men who responded to the call, "Follow me."

Apparently Jesus found no other way to mature his team and prepare them for service but the investment of personal time. And I doubt that any program of Christian discipleship or lay ministry today will develop mature Christian servants unless the leader provides large quantities of personal time, the heart of a humble servant and an unfailing measure of support and love for every member of the team.

The Gift of Time

As I look back over my years of ministry, it is clear to me that I did not teach others the principles of spiritual navigation mainly through my preaching, my teaching or even the modeling I attempted to do. I do hope some of that was effective. But it was the wonderful, long hours on late Saturday afternoons in my study with a dozen or more students, where together we shared our lives, supported each other in our desire to know Christ and do his will, and prayed for one another, that made the real difference. Sometimes I wonder if those were not the *only* times that truly brought honor to God. For me and for my colleagues, this interdependency, this long-on-time, mutual self-giving toward a common goal, shaped our lives.

Time is always a great gift of love. Jesus said, "A new commandment I give you: love one another. As I have loved you, so you must love one another. If you have love for one another, then all will know that you are my disciples" (Jn 13:34-35 TEV).

In the landmark book *The Making of a Leader* (NavPress, 1988, pp. 202-3), J. Robert Clinton writes that a leader is "a person with a God-given capacity, and with God-given responsibility to *influence* a specific group of God's people toward God's purposes for the group." Clinton continues,

> If the Lord were to make a statement to us, looking not only at the leadership gap but also at the present leaders, He might rephrase Matthew 9:36-38 as I have done:
>
>> When He saw the leaders, He was filled with dismay, because so many quit, so many were set aside, and so many were plateaued and directionless. They had lost their zest for leading. They had no clear philosophy or direction in their leadership. They were leaderless leaders. Then He said to His disciples, "The harvest is

plentiful, but the leaders with clear direction are few. Ask the Lord of the harvest, that He will send forth knowledgeable, discerning, and direction-oriented leader-laborers into His harvest."

Clinton then makes a wonderfully creative suggestion:

Wouldn't it be wonderful if ten or fifteen years from now the Lord Jesus could rephrase Matthew 9:36-38 in the following way?

When He saw the immensity of the work and the multitudes to be reached, He was not disheartened but was moved with joy because many leaders were meeting those needs and were continually raising up new leaders to meet the tremendous leadership challenge. He said, "Thank the Lord of the harvest, for He is giving harvest leaders, and they are leaders with direction and purpose."

If you are a spiritual commander, your crew needs to know that you know what you are doing. Many around you want to be leaders, but they have not sufficiently exposed themselves to the disciplines of leadership and have therefore disqualified themselves for service. Seek out those who are willing to learn the ropes, who are eager to launch out into the white water of conflict, and who are willing to sacrifice to be part of your team. It is my prayer that you will determine to continue to sail under divine command as you put into practice the Master's unfailing principles of leadership in your life and ministry.

5

Power for
Ministry:
Wind
in the Sails

LET EVERY CHRISTIAN UNDERSTAND

THAT WHEREVER TRUTH IS FOUND,

IT BELONGS TO HIS MASTER.

St. Augustine

T he beginning of my ministry was delayed and beset with many
difficulties. Some of my seminary classmates were launching out into
the ministry and establishing growing churches immediately upon grad-
uation. But I waited in embarrassed silence for more than three months
to be called to my first pastorate. I wondered if I would ever receive
the call to a church.

Finally one was entrusted to me, the South Hollywood Presbyterian
Church in Los Angeles, a congregation with a dwindling membership
and a solitary Saturday-morning employee. To make things worse, the
church was saddled with a building debt of thirty thousand dollars. A
five-thousand-dollar payment was due along with seventeen hundred
dollars in back interest on the loan. There was no prospect of clearing
any of these accounts during those Depression years. The bank officer

whose bank held the loan cautioned me against taking on the pastorate of the tiny congregation, because the bank was considering foreclosure.

I was concerned, but I'd also been called. I was eager to serve God with all I had to bring to my new ministry.

Gone Fishing

Let me back up a bit and describe for you the unconventional way I was chosen to become the pastor at South Hollywood. The three men on the pastor-seeking committee figured that taking their young prospect fishing would be one way to find out if he was the one to pastor their congregation. They reasoned that Jesus was looking for fishers of men, wasn't he? "If Munger catches his fish, we'll know he's our man."

To try out their theory, they took me for a day of deep-sea fishing off Santa Monica. We threw our lines over the side of the boat to see what we could get. All eyes were on my fishing line. "Is Munger going to catch anything? Will he be our man?" I could see them talking to each other, hoping I'd hook a mackerel or two.

In retrospect, I'm sure those good brothers didn't have a clue what to ask me about my faith, seminary experience, strategy for ministry or theology. But their purpose was right, and God used it. Though I'd never been deep-sea fishing in my life, I still caught more mackerel than the other three men combined. And I loved their goodhearted ingenuity and warm offer of friendship.

God's Hand on the Wheel

Despite all the challenges at hand, I knew South Hollywood was the place for me. What I would learn later was that in a most unusual and wonderful way, God was already preparing our little congregation to meet the opportunities of World War II, especially through ministry to the thousands of servicemen who would be pouring into Los Angeles and Hollywood. In the providence of God I was placed in the best possible setting for a beginner in pastoral leadership.

From my present perspective, I am awed at what God was beginning to do in my life. I was surrounded by great churches, great preachers, great spiritual youth movements and conferences, many of them strongly evangelical and biblical. A strong network of evangelical leadership encouraged me to grow spiritually, thus expanding and stimulating my understanding and doing of God's work.

Stewart McLennan (pastor of Hollywood Presbyterian Church), Henrietta Mears, Louis Evans Sr., Roy Creighton and Louis Talbot were models of ministry for me—all people whom I came to know personally. During my nine years at South Hollywood I also came in contact with what would later become the major evangelical parachurch organizations—institutions such as the Navigators, Wycliffe Bible Translators, the National Association of Evangelicals, Westmont College; then came Christian Endeavor, InterVarsity, Gospel Light Press, and later the Japanese Evangelical Society and many more. Through these organizations and their Christ-centered leadership I experienced Christ's presence. Further brightening the environment of ministry, a number of my Princeton teammates were neighbors and colleagues in ministry. But of all the spiritual input I received, none was more stimulating and helpful than the Hollywood fellowship under the able leadership of Henrietta Mears, God's gift to so many of us and especially to me as a beginner in Christian service.

During this time God also blessed me with the incomparable gift of a beloved wife. Without Edie my heart, longing for love, would not have been fulfilled—nor could the following years of service have been realized. Later two beautiful daughters were given to us to render completeness to an already happy home.

Family bonds are indispensable for anyone endeavoring to do ministry today, given the complexities of life as we now know them. I'm sure a few monastic types are somehow able to minister in a single role, but in my experience that is increasingly difficult and filled with problems. I needed the gift of a supportive, loving home as my foundation for the challenges of the ministry yet to come.

Setting Out to Sea

The first Sunday I preached, we scoured the congregation to find enough men to take the offering—not that we needed too many to carry the plates, for they were neither heavy nor full. When I saw that we couldn't even get a quorum of ushers, I knew we were in trouble. It was a church of older, relatively uninvolved parishioners, with only a few young couples in sight. The only reason as many as eighty adults were present for that first sermon was that my family and some Mount Hermon friends wanted to be on hand for my first pastoral performance. If those relatives and friends had not made the effort to come, there would have been even more empty pews.

I don't remember what I preached on that day, but my family thought I was great. Somehow I got started on my voyage, ready and willing to brace up for whatever winds might come my way.

As a young minister I had to learn some new navigational principles fast. Moody had introduced me to the basic manual of seamanship; Princeton had been my Annapolis, where I'd been allowed to take partial command in a few quiet harbors. But now I was on the high seas, commanding my first ship and not very skilled in working with my equally unskilled crew.

The Beginning of Growth

Soon after my arrival, there was some initial growth among the young people at South Hollywood, and this encouraged me greatly. Working with the adults was a greater challenge, but there too our congregation grew.

After the honeymoon period passed, though, there came a time when the church's growth and expansion leveled off. Instead of navigating prudently through these troubled waters, I quickly found myself in a spiritual storm.

I was twenty-six years old, and I possessed the eager heart of a young officer. But I learned one thing quickly: change is difficult for those who are settled in their ways. Believers without a life-changing experience with Christ are uncomfortable around younger people who have different ideas along with a vital experience of Christ. Established leaders tend to be threatened by younger, more venturesome Christians who want to make a difference. The result is tension. One day I would learn to prepare for change by making sure the older members knew they were loved and deeply valued by their pastor. Unfortunately, that wisdom came later.

Refusing to Deal with the Issues

In my first turn at the helm I didn't know how to handle conflict. I was afraid of it. I went out of my way to avoid the unpleasantness of any difficult situation, hoping that God would somehow bail me out and eliminate my responsibility for dealing with thorny issues. As struggles mounted in a variety of areas, my strategy was simply to pray more and redouble my efforts in other ministries. Then, after I had served three years at South Hollywood, a crisis came.

Our choir director, the most gifted and enthusiastic member of our new leadership team, was an experienced Christian who loved Christ and our young people. At the time she was tutoring young people from other areas of the city in music, offering these enthusiastic young musicians a major role in our small church choir. To me, this was a marvelous gift. The results of her efforts were phenomenal. Not only did the choir provide the congregation with high-quality music, it also attracted large numbers of participants, young and old. Within a year the choir was producing light opera concerts and performing in a sanctuary crowded with members, friends and neighbors. I sensed we were on our way. Our director's participation in worship added excitement, joy and an awareness that it *was* possible to put new wine into old wineskins.

But conflict was brewing. A new person arrived on the scene: a Bible teacher who told fascinating stories and unearthed information about the Old Testament that I had never heard in all my theological studies. Our choir director was so influenced by him and his gift of teaching that she opened her home for others to hear him speak. Of course many young people and adults crowded in to hear him.

In August of that year I was away on vacation. Upon my return, the choir director asked if this teacher could teach an adult Bible class on Sunday mornings before church, since there was no adult class at that time. But some investigation into the teacher's past revealed that no church had allowed him to minister with them for any length of time. He had neither credentials nor recommendations, and wherever he had been he had repeatedly asked for donations to support his teaching ministry. That less-than-glowing report on the teacher was enough for our group of elders. One of them felt that he was devious.

Still, the choir director was insistent. The tone of her voice, the set of her chin and the flash of her eyes warned me, "Back away!"

Princeton had not prepared me for what was about to happen. I had limited interpersonal skills and no background in counseling. I knew there was a problem but hoped the action of the elders would take care of it. Yet at the deepest level I sensed it was my responsibility.

I should have thought to visit the choir director at home and express my appreciation for all she was doing. I should have complimented her for the marvelous changes we were seeing not only among our young people but in the church as a whole. I then could easily have said, "You know, we have a problem. What can we do to resolve it?"

I may have been viewed by those around me as knowledgeable, mature and confident, but inwardly I struggled with immaturity and insecurity. I chose the modus operandi of cowardice and suggested that the elders take action on the problem instead of dealing with it myself. My action was not only unwise but also unbiblical. Matthew 5:24-26 reminds us, "First go and be reconciled to your brother. . . . Settle matters quickly with your adversary." Responsible leadership takes initiative to do the difficult in healing relationships. I flunked that test.

Sadly, the result was that the choir director felt unfairly treated by her pastor, who had made no effort to talk with her and take her cause seriously. She sensed she was no longer wanted or needed and quickly made plans to leave the church. When she left, most of the choral and youth leadership left with her.

Learning to Face Conflict

It was Saturday evening. I sat with four or five elders before the quarterly Sunday-morning Communion service as we prayed for the following day's services, a practice we had recently introduced. Crushed by the burden of conflict, I knew I needed God's forgiveness. I needed the director's forgiveness. I needed to confess that I had not been courageous, obedient or loving.

In the intimacy of that fellowship of prayer, I simply opened the floodgates of the heart and let my cry pour out. I confessed the true state of the situation. I was a big part of the problem. I needed God's forgiveness and the courage to try to make matters right. I said to the elders, "Please pray for me. I want to see the choir director this week and ask her forgiveness."

I found that being open and truthful did not mean I forfeited my position of pastoral authority. By God's grace I had made confession to the right people at the right time. Together we were given a fresh touch of God's peace and gracious provision. With confidence, we could place the matter in his safekeeping.

One of the younger elders put his arm around me as we left the room. "It's great to know that you're human like the rest of us," he said. (I assure you, it was no great surprise to me!) His response to my confession joined us as one in Christ at the deepest level of forgiveness—at the foot of the cross. Our friendship was firm and fast from then on.

But I was still fearful. Going through with my resolve was one of the toughest assignments I have had placed on me. But I did visit the former choir director, and the words finally came out: "I'm sorry—forgive me. I should have talked it over with you first." Her response was, "I'm sorry too. If you'd come to me sooner, I might not have left." In spite of the pain, a great peace began to settle in my heart. I sensed that God was pleased. The choir director did go her way, but I think she did so in peace. Our friendship was later restored, with warm family ties. The choir suffered, but over time the grace of God brought healing and restoration. Before long, new life and new leadership emerged—and new maturity for me.

I learned three unforgettable lessons during this painful leg of my voyage. First, go to the person yourself. Seek reconciliation. Second, confession to the proper person(s) is the fastest way to God's forgiveness, peace and the healing of relationships. Third, the supporting prayer of others empowers the process of reconciliation and healing.

Time of Trial

Lessons had been learned, forgiveness received, relationships finally restored—but all was still not well in the congregation. A painful period followed our choir director's departure. The loss of our gifted, energetic musician, her two talented daughters and her loyal followers left a void impossible to fill. The absence of a choir full of young voices lifting joyful hearts in praise made each worship service seem dull and heavy to me. Even my sermons seemed drained of life and without reality.

At times I felt hypocritical preaching about love, joy and peace when I myself was discouraged, depressed and defeated. I felt like Peter on Galilee with the little boat swamped and slowly going down. I could only cry to the Master, "Don't you care, Lord, if we perish?" Our little congregation seemed to be going down and under. Sunday attendance declined from 225 to 200 or less. My soul was joyless. I could see no way out. The confidence with which I had begun three years earlier was gone.

At times I gave serious thought to running off to a foreign mission field. Yes, I would do that. I would get on a sailing ship, cross great waters and convert a few heathen. I could then come back and tell moving stories of God's grace, perhaps thrill great audiences—and in the process escape my pain. Then I would wake up and recognize that such a "noble" escape would be less than noble and would really be only one more exercise in futility.

Nothing was working for me, not even my long hours of devotional study and earnest prayer. I knew I had the way, the truth and the life, but I did not have the power to live it out or to share it. First of all, I was hurting my Savior and my Friend. I was neither salt nor light. I was feeling empty of faith, hope and spiritual life. I was a miserable representation of what a Christian ought to be—a contradiction of the very gospel I was preaching.

Addressing the Inner Turbulence

In the early fall of 1939, with my ship becalmed and drifting, I attended a pastors' retreat at the newly established Forest Home Christian Conference Center in the San Bernardino Mountains. The conference was for pastors who wanted a renewal of spiritual life for themselves and their congregations. The speaker, Armin Gesswein, had just returned from an extended visit to Norway, where he had witnessed a spiritual awakening of apostolic power, with manifestations of the Holy Spirit and unprecedented, dramatic conversions. With wide-eyed amazement, he had seen a reliving of the book of Acts. Then Norway had been occupied by Nazi troops. The first phase of World War II was beginning.

Gesswein's message to us was "Let Americans take heed. Prepare spiritually for the coming conflict. Be filled and equipped with the power of God!"

Like a flash of lightning, the truth hit me. That was exactly what I needed—the power and equipping of the Holy Spirit. A pastor and his people needed the wind of the Spirit to fill their sails and their souls if they were to move out of the doldrums.

I felt compelled to talk to the speaker. He gave me time and graciously listened to my sad story. I'm sure I fumbled all over my words. But Armin listened. He sensed I had heard all I needed to know and was aware that my heart was being prepared. And Armin would trust Christ to do his work in me in his way and in his time. He simply said, "Bob, when you're ready, God is going to meet you."

I could have kicked his shins. I was so ready I would have jumped from a window if I felt God had told me to! But Armin promised he would pray for me. He did. And he still does, thank God, after more than fifty years of prayer partnership.

It dawned on me that I had been failing for the same reason the disciples had failed before Pentecost. So starting with Genesis 1:1, I began reading through the entire Bible, marking every reference to the Holy Spirit. By the time I had reached John 7:37 at the beginning of a new year, I was battering at the gates of heaven, praying earnestly for the Spirit's power. I was desperately thirsting for the promised rivers of living water.

I decided I would have it out with God. Either he would equip me with the power of his Spirit, or I would find some other vocation. I probably would have lacked the courage to follow through on my threat, but at the time I felt desperately determined.

Read, Munger, Read!
One evening I went into a small room in the back of the church, away from phones, people and distractions. I wanted to be alone. I would thrash things out with God. No one else was in the building. All the lights were out.

I knelt and prayed, "Lord, either you meet me tonight and give me deliverance, or I'll leave the ministry. I'm not going to stand here and be a hypocrite talking about your grace and love."

Then the Lord seemed to say to me, *Read this, Bob Munger! It's important. Just open it and look!* No doubt these words were an echo of the conversion experience of St. Augustine. According to his *Confessions,* Augustine was moved to a life-changing experience with God as he heard a sentence spoken by children who were playing on the other side of a wall. He didn't even see the children; he simply heard them say, "Take up and read."

I was sure God was directing me to the Bible, but where in the Bible was I to read? I knew exactly where my well-worn Scofield Bible would open—right to Isaiah 53. It always opened at that chapter. I felt like saying, "Look, I know that passage well. What do you want me to know?"

But the impulse within continued. I turned on the light, and my Bible opened not to Isaiah 53 but to Isaiah 54. The words I saw looming before me could not have been more personal or more direct communication with God if spoken audibly. I read,

> More are the children of the desolate. . . . Enlarge the place of thy
> tent, and let them stretch forth the curtains of thy habitations: spare
> not, lengthen thy cords, and strengthen thy stakes; For thou shalt
> break forth on the right hand and on the left; and thy seed shall
> inherit the Gentiles, and make the desolate cities to be inhabited.
> Fear not; for thou shalt not be ashamed: neither be thou confounded;
> for thou shalt not be put to shame. . . . For a small moment have I
> forsaken thee; but with great mercies will I gather thee. In a little
> wrath I hid my face from thee for a moment; but with everlasting
> kindness will I have mercy on thee, saith the LORD thy Redeemer. (vv.
> 1-4, 7-8 KJV)

It was a breakthrough of God's grace. I was heard. He was answering. God was going to open up streams of living water in the parched desert of my soul.

I began to pray with expectation, even to the extent of praising God for what he was *going* to do in my life. I prayed, "I don't know how you're going to handle it, Lord, but you're going to do it. Somehow you're going to enlarge the tent, and you're going to remove the disgrace and use me after all. You hid your face for a moment, but it was only for a moment."

Conversion of the Unconscious

I felt somehow I had become party to a solemn blood covenant, like the one the Lord God had made with Abraham. I had offered to God all I was and all I had. He—Father, Son and Holy Spirit—had accepted the offer and given word that my prayer for an energizing of the Holy Spirit would be fulfilled. This was, to me, more than a simple reaching out of my hand that he might draw me up out of the darkness of those angry waves into his love and saving life. It was more than signing up for lifesaving service under my Friend, Savior and Captain. It went much deeper and further.

In the words of the late E. Stanley Jones, it was "the conversion of the unconscious" as well as a conscious captivating of the core of my soul. God would take responsibility for everything. My job was to let him do it, to trust him and do what he said. I would never again go through that feeling of conscious loss of his presence. I had stated the one thing I needed above all from God, and that was a smile on the face of Jesus, my Savior, Friend and Lord. With that I could be at his service anywhere, doing anything. The peace of assurance filled my heart.

I saw my need to let go of dependence on myself, my knowledge, my abilities, my prayer and my faith to God through the Holy Spirit. A massive movement of trust from self to the Savior would be involved. Had not Jesus said, "Without me you can do nothing"? I knew it was true. In spite of our best efforts—in spite of *my* best efforts—I could not bring spiritual life into being, neither in myself or through myself. God alone could impart genuine life, and the Holy Spirit was his means.

My brokenness had produced openness. All the apertures of my soul were open for God's control. I wanted myself displaced to the glory of God. Perhaps the Holy Spirit had not been given to me because I had not been ready to have Jesus Christ glorified in everything in my life.

I can't say any dramatic changes accompanied these profound new insights, but I finally had a spirit of hopeful expectation. I discovered I had to be broken from my preconceived, fleshly ideas of power and to shift from confidence in myself to confidence in my Captain. We all know Jesus said, "Without me you can do nothing," but I'm convinced most of us don't believe it until God *shows* us we can do nothing apart from him and his power. Only when we hit that nothingness are we broken.

Six weeks of eager, expectant prayer and praise followed. Armin kept in touch with me during this period and asked me to join a pastor's prayer fellowship with him on a Monday morning. I wasn't too excited about going, nor was I comfortable with the denominational backgrounds of those he told me usually attended. Besides, I had just been through a most strenuous weekend—a countywide Christian Endeavor gathering with four thousand young people at the Long Beach Auditorium. My part had been to instruct more than one hundred of those who were seeking the Lord after the concluding invitation. It was exciting, but I was exhausted. So I declined.

But Armin quietly persisted, and I'm grateful he did. As I hung up the receiver, I remembered the covenant I had made a few weeks before to be wholly God's. Reluctantly, I decided to go.

"Munger, I'm Speaking to You!"

The speaker at that Monday-morning gathering was a man named Morrisey, an excellent Bible teacher who had been a student at Biola when R. A. Torrey was president. Morrisey began his devotional by reflecting on Torrey's thoughts on the Holy Spirit. He talked of the importance of understanding the various steps of becoming acquainted with the third Person of the Trinity and of what it meant to be filled with the Spirit and to be anointed for ministry. He was quoting from his personal conversation with Torrey. He said, "If you think of the Holy Spirit as a mere influence or power, as so many even among Christian people do today, then your thought will constantly be 'How can I get hold of the Holy Spirit and use it?' But if you think of him in the New Testament way, as a personal deity, your thought will be, 'How can the Holy Spirit get hold of me and work through me?' "

Once again it was the word of authority, but the speech was that of a friend: *Bob, I'm speaking to you. Get this!* Just a few days before, I had been reading John 7:37-39: "If any man thirst, let him come unto me, and drink. He that believeth on me, as the scripture hath said, out of his [inward being] shall flow rivers of living water. (But this spake he of the Spirit, which they that believe on him should receive: for the Holy Ghost was not yet given; because that Jesus was not yet glorified)" (KJV).

I knew I had received the water of life. But a trickle was only enough to make me thirsty for more. I had not yet experienced rivers of life-giving water flowing from me to others. The prospect of experiencing authentic joy and power through the Holy Spirit, imparted on the night of crisis six weeks before, surged into my soul. My heart beat fast with expectation. Perhaps here, at this time, I would by faith be able to drink deeply of that water of life.

Afraid but Hopeful

One day as I prayed with Dick Halverson at a Forest Home gathering, he poured out his heart in a way that perfectly expresses what I wanted that Monday morning. He prayed, "Lord, put me on like an old glove and use me any way you want."

I think of it this way. Suppose you were to pick up an old, weathered garden glove or work glove—one that has been out in the weather or buried on a beach. Say that you wanted to use it but found it as hard as a rock. Yet picking it up, shaking out the sand and gradually working it over, you discover you can soften it up until the glove is finally ready to be filled out to the fingertips. In God's love and grace, he had been working me over for some time—much like a weather-beaten old glove. Now I was ready to let the glove be filled to the fingertips. I wanted to be put on for his intended use, which was to serve him, love him, share his grace and enhance his glory.

Morrisey's subject that morning was "How to Be Filled with the Spirit." I knew he was speaking to me. Was this the moment when I should openly and boldly ask God to do it? Suppose nothing happened. Suppose I was given the gift of glossolalia. Then what would I do? For me, it was a step of enormous venture and consequence.

The time soon came for us to pray. About a dozen of us knelt in a circle. Would I share my condition? Would I admit my desperation? Did I dare pray publicly for God to give me a special anointing and infilling of the Spirit of God, even though it might mean a radical change in the direction and association of my ministry? I had covenanted in writing before God in that crisis night that I would do anything, everything, go anywhere.

It was a *kairos* (crisis) moment. Finally it was my time to pray. I told the gathered Christian brothers that I needed to be filled with the Spirit and asked them to pray for me. They did—earnestly, lovingly and with warm faith. Then I prayed, reminding God from Scripture of our covenant relationship and what he had already promised to give me for his glory.

When I finished praying, the brother next to me, a big man whom I did not know but whose loving concern I could feel, put his arm around me and said, "Lord, help Bob's unbelief!" That was a bit hard to take, but I took it! I had often told inquirers that we receive Christ not by feelings but by faith in his person and promise. Now, suddenly, my own faith came alive. With a holy boldness I told God the Father, Son and Holy Spirit that I was now receiving all of him and all that was meant in John 7:37-39. I thanked God that he was doing what I had asked of him. Now I knew for certain he would glorify Jesus Christ somehow even in me.

The Word of God Coming to Life

On the way out, Armin asked me, "Do you think God heard your prayer?"

I said, "I hope so, because I feel confident I've done everything the Lord has been asking me to do. I can think of nothing more. The next step is up to him."

"That's good," Armin said. "Keep on thanking him."

I went home that morning with the strong sense that God had heard my prayer. I sat down alone in my study and reflected on the morning. I had enough assurance to praise God, and I quietly thanked him for the peace that had finally settled in my soul. He would do what I had asked, and my struggle would be over. My mood was open, receptive and expectant, not only to *receive* the Holy Spirit but also to recognize that the Spirit of God was now actually resident in my life and in full control of my heart. I belonged to God fully, body and soul. He would do the rest.

I never did speak in tongues, nor did I experience any immediate manifestations. But I did know that the simple inner witness of the Spirit had come to me and that he was in charge of my body, his temple.

That evening, as I gave a devotional talk to a group of young couples at a summer evening picnic, I sensed a new freedom and fullness of the presence of God. Whether the others noticed it I don't know. But from that time on I have been aware that he is the resident, indwelling Lord of my life and that he will be with me *forever* (Jn 15:16).

For the next few years I wanted to tell everybody about my experience, whether they wanted to hear it or not. But I had to be careful how I talked about it, how I shared it with my congregation, friends and family. I'm sure many of them would have misunderstood, feeling that Munger had become unstable and had gone off the deep end. Remember, in those years the charismatic movement had not yet touched mainline denominations.

But I found the Bible coming alive to me in a new way. The Scriptures had begun to speak to me when I first came to know Christ personally in 1932. Now the communication was not just a matter of *seeing* but also of *hearing*. It was as if I were in the living presence of the One addressing me. The communication was more direct. The Holy Spirit was in my heart. It was as if I had put on new spiritual spectacles and could see Christ clothed with cosmic power.

I began to believe a motto I'd recently seen on the wall of a neighboring church: "Jesus Christ is here; anything can happen!" As I preached and served, I sensed at times that living water was flowing. There was a new freedom, a new authority, a new conviction of Scripture as the Word of God, a new reality. My sermons took on a freshness, carrying with them the conviction of authoritative truth.

As if by some miracle, books on the dynamics of the spiritual life suddenly challenged and blessed me. I could not get enough of the powerful biographies and writings of Andrew Murray, George Müller, D. L. Moody and A. T. Pearson, to name a few. Each confirmed my own spiritual experience.

I had already learned that "man shall not live by bread alone," and I was now feeding my soul on rich spiritual food. If food is not assimilated, it does little good in nourishing the body. Now the Holy Spirit was alive and active in my life, enabling me to appropriate and assimilate his truth, then to share it and satisfy the hunger of others. I felt energized with his truth, authority and power through personal conversation with the living Lord, speaking from Scripture.

The Right Word, the Right Accent
The writer Joseph Conrad once said, "Give me the right word with the right accent and I can take the world." God had given me the right word. I also had the right accent: the written Word of God, the Scripture, the truth. The truth of God's Word and the gospel had been explained to me at Moody. Then I studied the Bible in even greater depth and was trained for its enunciation and propagation at Princeton. There was no

question about it. I had the right accent, and I knew God's Word was true. That truth was confirmed again and again by the response of our young people and others to the gospel. The validation of that truth strengthened my confidence.

My prayer life was also liberated, fed by the pure oxygen of the Holy Spirit promised in Romans 8:26. He became a marvelous "help" in my weakness. I was now being granted a conscious personal hearing with the triune God. I was enrolled in God's school of intercessory prayer. In this school all know they are only beginners being taught first to seek God's will and listen carefully to his Word, then to intercede in his name and for his glory.

Prayer began to impart power. Prayer became real. It made a difference in the world around me, the church and my own life. In the school of prayer I moved from petition—cries for help—to conversation— intimate fellowship and sharing—to intercession. At times I found myself becoming an advocate before the bar of God's covenant promises, pleading that his word of promise be reconciled with his word of fidelity, truth and love.

Today I'm still in the lower grades. I have much more to learn. But I'm grateful that I know more now than when I began the Christian life. For me prayer is more than beneficial—not only for my ministry but also for the cause of Christ throughout the world. As oxygen was necessary for my body, so prayer became necessary to my soul. My prayer life was liberated and authenticated.

Once the accent was right, the Holy Spirit projected God's Word through my sermons with a new, penetrating power. From the time of that initial experience with the Spirit of God, it seemed to me that everything around me made a sudden, quantitative leap forward. My spiritual energy abounded. My limited gifts as a communicator would now be fed supercharged fuel. God was doing things only he could do. As Jesus opened the minds of the two on the road to Emmaus, so he seemed to be opening the minds of those who heard my preaching and teaching. People were understanding the Scriptures and discovering there was indeed a living Lord.

It was not dramatic. I did not change my style or manner of preaching, but here and there people began to hear the truth and trust God in new ways. They were venturing out into uncharted waters. The little two-by-four world of my ministry was expanding. The new life given to me was producing new life in others.

Now that the Holy Spirit was in control of my life, I sensed my heart and body had been changed. I had been indwelt by Jesus Christ through the new birth, but now was also anointed of the Spirit for the work he entrusted me to do.

As the clouds of war flashed lightning over Europe and the roar of battle intensified, spiritual victories were being won in our membership. The ordinary had become a theater of extraordinary happenings. The supernatural became amazingly more natural. Conflicts continued to occur. The enemy was not conquered, but we had discovered a faith that overcomes the world, the flesh and the devil.

Quantum Leap

I was proud of the way our young people responded to the challenges of war, especially in maintaining Christian convictions and character in the midst of many trials and temptations. By 1945 over one hundred from our congregation were in uniform; two had been killed in action, and one had endured four years as a Japanese POW. I treasure a book of some forty letters in which these brave men and women express appreciation for the touch of God given them through the church. These people were good soldiers of the cross as well as of Uncle Sam.

Under the clouds of war we saw new life in the congregation. Seekers came to us, and leaders began to emerge. The membership rose to 750. In time the church had a full-time secretary with a part-time director of our church school. In those days associate pastors were rare for congregations of that size. Yet steadily our people matured and multiplied, with good leadership given voluntarily and selflessly to the Lord.

We always felt we were in a crisis of need: first to retire the debt, second to provide adequate programs, and third to be more engaged in sharing the gospel and loving our neighbors. There were always problems and perils to be faced. Yet somehow God always saw us through.

I learned there are times when God delights to use inadequate and unprepared instruments. Samson once picked up the nearest object, the jawbone of a donkey, and used it to defeat many enemies (Judg 16:15). It amazes me that God often seems to use the most unlikely and least positioned congregation in a city to do something unique and beautiful for the glory of God.

To the Troops with Love

A major lesson of the war years was that through faith and prayer, the Holy Spirit empowers God's people in ministry for evangelism. This was powerfully demonstrated through a ministry to military personnel, seventy thousand of whom flooded Los Angeles and Hollywood every weekend for rest and recreation. Our outreach to soldiers began in a most amazing way.

We were not located near the center of Hollywood, where those thousands of service personnel thronged the USOs, the streets and theaters for entertainment. That's why I'm proud of how our church pursued its unprecedented opportunity to touch the lives of these young men for Christ.

This ministry to our troops started out simply enough. A group of seven mothers met at the church every Friday morning to pray for their own sons who had gone overseas. One Sunday morning a faithful member of this band of praying women was driving to church with her husband when she saw three servicemen walking along Sunset Boulevard near Vine in Hollywood. It was early. There was obviously nothing for the boys to do. This godly woman asked her husband to stop the car as she leaned out the window and said, "You men look like you don't have a lot going on this morning. Why not come with us to church? Our people are friendly, the church is comfortable, and we'll bring you back at 12:15. I have two sons in the service. I'd love to have you with us. Why not come along!"

Well, with an invitation like that, how could they refuse! Sitting on a church pew at the moment seemed better than wearily ambling along the deserted streets of Hollywood. The men jumped in the car and came to the service, an event that marked the beginning of an exciting ministry. The idea spread quickly throughout the congregation and it didn't take long for others to join in the opportunity. During the next six months, after nearly every service, a group of servicemen met with me, seeking to know Christ personally. We prayed for them, gave them follow-up materials, and commended them to the grace and care of God. As many as fifty men in uniform would be crowded into the church on a Sunday morning, and in earnest response to the invitation, more than half would usually squeeze into the little prayer room to receive instruction on how to know Christ personally—and to have him with them through the dangers and testing ahead.

During this time, the seven mothers continued their prayer vigil. Of course, others now had joined them in bringing servicemen to worship. It was without doubt one of the most dramatic examples of answered prayer I have ever known—one that helped shape my understanding of the connection between intercession and evangelism for years to come.

There is one more person I must thank for his prayers for me, his lifetime of friendship, and the way he helped me shape my world to see a lost humanity. He also helped me catch the vision for trained, mature disciples to fulfill God's saving purpose. That man was Dawson Trotman, founder of the Navigators. During the winter of 1945, Daws gathered around him six or eight of us to pray for those we knew in military action. He had the names of hundreds of servicemen at his fingertips. The Navigator ministry was strongly underway.

When Daws told me the time of our prayer meeting would be from five until seven a.m., I could not believe he was expecting *me* to join the fellowship. I was about to refuse the invitation to be one of this party of intercessors until he told me people such as Dick Hillis and others who at that time were outstanding, effective Christian servants, working with the military in various ways, would be attending. There were also some wonderful lay brothers, about eight of us in all. I had never gotten up at 4:00 a.m. to get to a 5:00 a.m. prayer meeting even *once* in my life, let alone made a commitment to do it every week. This was going to be a struggle. But inside I knew something tremendous was going to happen in those prayer meetings, and I had better figure out a way to get there and not miss out.

Somehow I managed to stagger there every Friday for that winter and spring. I was impressed with Daws's careful, systematic, organized approach. Every week, each of us would bring the names of our young men in the military. Toward the end of our time together, we began to pray not only for our service personnel but also for the countries and locations where they were serving. In due course, we began to pray for those areas where there was such great need, such as Southeast Asia, where much of the fighting was going on, and the countries of Europe. We were praying that God would lead some of the men who were now mature, disciplined, dedicated to serving their country even unto death, to give God that same quality of commitment.

This kind of prayer was not exactly easy, nor was it enjoyable. It was hard work. We kept each other awake and alive because of the serious-ness of the purpose for which we were praying. We lost all sense of counting numbers or who the people were, at least I did, because it was a joint effort, and there was a cause that was as important as the physical combat going on.

Some six years later, Dawson Trotman and his wife joined Edie and me for a three-day winter break in our little cottage at Mount Hermon. We had no agenda except for them to get a break, and then to talk with them about what was going on in the world and for the cause of Christ as we understood it.

Daws said something I'll never forget. "Bob, my secretary researched some astonishing answers to our prayers for servicemen recently." He then listed several countries we had intentionally prayed for—countries in and near the battle zones. He said that there was now a full-time person serving Christ with the Navigators in each one of the fifteen or more countries we had prayed for. In half a dozen countries there were two missionaries. *And that was within six years of the time when we were praying so earnestly.* I do not regard that as a coincidence. There was an intention to be sure on the part of the Navigators to do that very thing, but I've always felt those early morning prayer hours had a major part to play in the explosive expansion of the Navigator ministry.

Dawson Trotman helped to deepen my commitment and drove me to excel as a Christian disciple. God in his great mercy once again became alive in my life. The Holy Spirit was giving me the joy of being used in God's great cause with the assurance of his ultimate victory. While never in uniform, I was privileged to engage in frontline spiritual warfare with veteran intercessors. It was an experience of intercessory prayer with tangible results and biblical principles of ministry. I discovered *it is as important to talk to God about people as to talk to people about God.*

Sharing Christ in Today's War Zones

Today, as we approach the close of this millennium, the spiritual battle for the minds, hearts and loyalty of men and women continues between the forces of light and darkness. In those early years of World War II, I learned the powerful connection between prayer and visible results. The same strategies work today.

I learned that the best way to get people from Sunset Boulevard inside the church to turn to God was *through the ministry of intercession.* Only a handful of people were engaged in this ministry, but it doesn't take many to move the hand of God. For us, it happened through the lives of ordinary people of God with burdened spirits and persistence in prayer who never stopped pouring out their hearts before the Lord whom they loved and trusted. For this small group of prayer warriors, their ministry was a high calling of great urgency. They devoted themselves to it around the clock, forever putting feet to their own petitions. Times have changed, but the goodness of God, the efficacy of prayer and the power of love, quickened by the Holy Spirit, have not. There are no impossibilities for the will of God even in this day of intense spiritual conflict.

Evangelism is supernatural work. It cannot be done without the power of the Holy Spirit. Plans and efforts without earnest prayer and strong faith do not bring positive results. But persistent, heartfelt prayer lifted in the name of Jesus Christ and for his concerns holds wonderful power.

What about our various ministries today? Who is walking on the Sunset Boulevards of our communities? How are we doing in our late-twentieth-century war zones? Whom are you and I missing simply because we are looking the other way? Are we involved in causes bigger than ourselves? Are we aware of today's casualties of war—the wars of drugs, divorce, prejudice, ignorance and abuse? Are we as leaders making a critical difference in the lives of others? No one needs a formal theological education to make an impact as a Christian. Just as Jesus chose to use nonprofessionals to carry out his mandate, he will continue to use us and our dominant desires to extend the kingdom, whether we've been trained theologically or not. Our mandate is simply to pay attention to the crushing need around us and to respond to that physical and spiritual need in Jesus' name.

The late Ray Stedman used to say, "The best place for a resurrection is in a graveyard." I hope you view today's social and spiritual graveyard crises as ministry opportunities to love men and women, boys and girls to Jesus and into the kingdom.

Toward the end of my years at South Hollywood, God was blessing us richly. The war had made us tough, sensitive, gentle, resilient and fully reliant on our Captain, Jesus Christ. We lived with weekly announcements of lost lives, shattered hopes and broken dreams. But our ship was afloat and on course; the crew had become adept and well trained for service. Our congregation was never large, but it was always willing to develop a deeper relationship with the Father, to recognize the power of the Holy Spirit and to make Jesus Christ known to all.

"You Haven't Suffered"

My message to today's Christian leaders is that we need this same perspective and this same indwelling of the Holy Spirit in our lives. It is the Spirit alone who will lead us to repentance. It isn't that God doesn't love us; he just cannot and will not bless us when we blatantly disregard his principles for living lives of righteousness.

While today's economy may be tough and our social problems difficult to understand, much less manage, we still have it soft. Most of us do not suffer and have never *really* suffered. Years ago a Fuller Seminary student asked German theologian Helmut Thielicke his impressions of America. He spoke three words: "You haven't suffered."

True, we at home knew little of the kind of suffering civilians in Europe went through as the war came to their villages and homes. Nightly bombings, starvation, the horrors of being overrun by the enemy—by comparison, our scarcity of meat and gasoline was trivial.

Yet the war years were challenging for the American people, both military and civilian. There were heroes in the air, at sea and in the trenches. There were heroes in our airplane factories, shipyards and victory gardens. And there were also heroes in the cause of Jesus Christ.

However, with the passing of time, the mood and motivation for sharing the good news has changed. Today, much of the drive is for grabbing and getting rather than giving; for security and comfort, not sacrifice; for self-interest rather than self-giving. Today, we want to be entertained, not enlightened. We find it easier to be sinful than sanctified. Many would rather be led than learn to lead with courage; would rather be dictated to than discipled; are more eager to embrace the pleasant and convenient than to *do the right thing.* The cults are growing because they are committed to a cause. Armies of religious and political fanatics are making great strides because they have laserlike goals and objectives.

Let's think about our own priorities. Are they in sync with Christ's call and provision? In my observation our clear purpose must be to develop members of the body to be like Christ and do his will, even when it calls for self-denial. These will be the Christians who are alive, effective in witness, growing and filled with excitement and joy. These will be— and are—the men and women whose faith and lives are real.

A Marxist's Commitment

Former communist leader Douglas Hyde puts it in perspective when he says in *Dedication and Leadership* (University of Notre Dame Press, 1966):

> The Communists make far bigger demands upon their people than the average Christian organisation would ever dare make. . . .They believe that if you make big demands upon people you will get a big response. So this is made a deliberate policy on their part. They never make a small demand if they can make a big one. . . . "Every Communist is a leader, every factory a fortress" is one of their slogans. But it is more than a slogan, it is an aim, and one which they set out very determinedly to achieve. The meaning behind the slogan is this: Each party member must be so trained that no matter where he may find himself he will be qualified to come forward and lead; and, when you have sufficient such members together in a given factory or within some particular organisation, they can make this a "fortress" for Communism. . . . Marx concluded his Communist Man-

ifesto with the words, "You have a world to win." Here is a tremendous aim. In material terms, one could hardly aim higher. . . . The Communist tutor is expected to remind himself over and over that he is not just concerned with passing knowledge to people. His aim is to equip them for action and to assist them in becoming leaders. (pp. 27, 29, 31, 74)

Are those few comments of Hyde enough to challenge us to evaluate our commitment to Jesus Christ? Is our slogan *We have a world to win?* Are we helping those around us equip themselves for action and assisting them in developing leadership roles for the even more challenging twenty-first century? God never has demanded productivity, but he's always wanted our availability. Can we become conspirators for good, actually helping create a *war effort* mentality in our ministries? During World War II no one built an airplane, a ship, a factory, a bridge or a bullet by himself or herself. It was a team effort, complete with all the pain, sacrifice, joy and sorrow. We did without because we knew it was for a noble cause.

To the Next Port of Entry

The ship *South Hollywood Presbyterian Church* was now at full sail, with a full passenger list and full cargo. Was it not time now for me to be given a new assignment? God had made our congregation vibrant and alive. The Holy Spirit had sensitized us to a world in need, and in his power we were helping to make a difference in the lives of others. But I knew I would not stay there indefinitely. Just as I had wondered why my first call was delayed after Princeton, once again I found myself becoming impatient that other doors had not yet opened for me. Would I ever learn to trust God and his timing?

I became increasingly aware that if God were to open the door to my home congregation in Berkeley, that would be a fulfillment of all God had been preparing me to be and do. I knew the church from the inside as a spiritual son of the congregation. I was familiar with its university setting and at home with its people. In the end, in fact, that would be the way God would lead. When the call did come, I knew it would be an exciting voyage, but little did I know I would be sailing into seas leading to so many boundless opportunities! They are the subject of the next chapter.

6
Mission:
A Mandate
for the
High Seas

THE LEADER WHO UNDERSTANDS

THE PRINCIPLE OF ENERGY IS AWARE OF

THE IMPORTANCE OF DEMONSTRATING

ENERGY BEFORE HIS FOLLOWERS.

THEY WILL NOT BE MORE ENTHUSIASTIC

THAN THE LEADER IS.

John Haggai, *Lead On!*

The exigencies of total war produced heroic leaders. Their names, too numerous to mention, will be remembered to the end of history: Omar Bradley, Winston Churchill, Franklin Roosevelt, George Patton, Douglas MacArthur, Jimmy Doolittle and so many more. At 8:15 a.m. on August 6, 1945, a B-29 dropped the atomic bomb on Hiroshima. The blast destroyed more than four square miles of the city and left seventy-one thousand dead or missing. Three days later, the United States dropped another atomic bomb, this time on the city of Nagasaki. Some forty thousand were killed, and one-third of the city was devastated. On August 14, 1945, the Japanese surrendered. With a formal surrender signed on September 2, aboard the battleship *Missouri* in Tokyo Bay, World War II officially came to an end.

One month earlier, I had left my parish in South Hollywood to take the reins as pastor of the First Presbyterian Church in Berkeley, California! It would be a new world for me and a congregation that was nursing its own war wounds as I entered my second and most important major mission. Our church would soon be playing a key role in a burgeoning national spirit—ready and, with God's help, willing to respond to the challenges of rebuilding a shelter of new opportunities and new safeguards against tyranny, oppression and evil.

I received my call to the First Presbyterian Church of Berkeley in the spring of 1945. Having hoped this opportunity might come one day, I looked forward to my new ministry with great anticipation. From the outset I had a strong sense of what lay ahead of me in Berkeley. I was heading into one of the most challenging intellectual and educational centers in the world.

Prepared by God

I never felt better about any call than this one at Berkeley. This exciting new opportunity seemed to have been designed by God for me from my birth. First, I had come home. This was the church of my youth; the congregation still contained friends from my boyhood days. I knew these people. I was familiar with the environment. I knew I could make a contribution. At the same time I looked back and developed an even deeper appreciation of the basic lessons confirmed during my nine years in South Hollywood. So many truths about my commitment to Christ had been validated for me. Christ had proved a trustworthy guide. I would be secure, faithfully following him, walking in the light. I was assured he would be with me in this new step even as he had been ever since I had put him in charge, that eventful night when I surrendered my vocation and location to God. He would handle the next unknown, humanly impossible leadership challenge *if* I would simply honor him and rely on him. That is exactly what he did through this trusting, willing servant in spite of my feeble but growing faith.

My faith in Scripture had also been strengthened. I had seen the Word of God quicken faith in Christ and enable a person to become well-rounded and mature in the Christian faith. I also had made the great discovery that God himself is the great worker, that getting the job done did not depend upon my abilities, influence, contacts or education. I had learned that it was *his* operation. My job was simply to have confidence in him. All this had come to be part of my very being through the experience with the Holy Spirit in 1940 and the transformation he graciously brought about at South Hollywood.

Two Validations of Intercessory Prayer

As I made the move toward Berkeley, I had been given a paradigm shift in my understanding of who the worker was in God's business and who I was—and wasn't. In my last years at Hollywood I saw God doing humanly impossible works in answer to intercessory prayer. For example, I had seen intercessory prayer work in evangelism, especially in the lives of our servicemen. Praying women and others would not let God forget our men and women overseas, nor would they forget the weekend warriors who wandered the streets of our own Hollywood.

Then, through Navigators founder Dawson Trotman and our early-morning fellowship, it was demonstrated to me how our intercessory prayers could actually shape the ministry of those who were involved in war. The ways of God are mysterious. My personal involvement in the crises of World War II, and the continuing spiritual warfare, showed me the truth that prayer really is effective. I think of men like Joe Kropff, one of our South Hollywood boys, and others whose lives were spared miraculously in the war, who went on to give their lives for the gospel in ministry or on the mission field. Not all of them did, of course, but enough to validate the principle of prayer and mission.

For the first time I was exposed to the impact of the gospel in a crosscultural or "foreign" mission. From my youth, missions had always played a great role in my understanding of Christian life and service. It was instilled early. But my trip to Mexico with Edie and Ed and Margaret Caldwell, colleagues in ministry, caused my heart to burn even more brightly for those in other countries without Christ. Against the background of appalling human need and suffering, I had seen the supernatural power of God in the process of transforming lives almost before my eyes.

I will never forget the light of God's love shining through the faces of those with nothing of this world's goods, yet who could lift their hearts in praise and joyful song to their Redeemer. I returned with renewed commitment to be a world Christian wherever God would place me. My assignment at Berkeley would be to advance this cause from the strategic home base of the Berkeley church. Looking back, I now see that God had long been in the process of preparing me for this new assignment. This gave me the certainty that I understood what he wanted me to do.

The Berkeley Mandate

During the month of August 1945, we had the opportunity to spend our vacation at Lake Tahoe in Tahoe Meadows. Our cottage was on the beach with a warm southwestern exposure. It looked out over the water toward Mount Talack. Our eldest daughter was only two years old, and she enjoyed playing in the sand with her three cousins. It was a delightful summer. Still, while we were enjoying those halcyon days at Tahoe, Europe was still reeling from the horror of war and bloodshed that had torn it apart. Japan was engaging us in the Pacific with great losses.

Suddenly the solitude of our Tahoe reverie was shattered with the detonation of the first nuclear bomb. In a flash, literally, we were catapulted into a new age in which the ultimate destruction might be the end of the world. It was now possible for human beings to annihilate themselves in one horrible nuclear conflagration. Even as I write these words, the horror of that moment makes my heart race as I see flash before me those terrible headlines, and the pictures of the victims of the first horrible nuclear blast.

We had more than a month in the mountains before returning to Berkeley to begin our ministry. I took advantage of the mornings to be alone for a few hours while Edie and our little daughter were happily engaged in other things. I would drive a ways and then walk to a secluded spot, high on a hillside that overlooked the lake, and sit in the shade of a tree. There I did some thinking and praying. There I would ask God what my real assignment was to be in the days ahead.

The more I prayed, the greater and bolder my faith became. Instead of my becoming depressed or anxious by the catastrophic perils unfolding in world events, God widened my perspective for *reaching* that world with the message of his Son. I already knew the life-changing power of the gospel message and the truth of God's Word, the Bible, when shared by the power of the Holy Spirit through a united people. God had demonstrated to me that he was able to do above all that I asked or thought (Eph 3:20). My new assignment would offer to me newer and larger opportunities to lift higher the only Savior of the world and to do his will for people everywhere who were in such desperate need.

One morning I opened the Scriptures to Isaiah 54—old, familiar verses regarding the promise of power through the Holy Spirit. Now, however, I found myself reading the words of the prophet with a profound sense of opportunity. I could not shake the mandate of the second and third verses of the chapter. They instructed me to strengthen the stakes and lengthen the cords. These words commissioned me both in my personal life and in my relation to the congregation I was to serve. I was challenged to reach out farther than the people had ever reached before—to embrace an entire world for Christ. I also noticed the words "Your descendants will possess the nations and will settle the desolate towns." Our obedience would issue in God's action. There would be results even in far nations and desolate cities (Is 54:3). In my mind, I began to see God's people carrying the torch of his truth into far lands and dark corners. It would be done through the ministry of others, some of whom, by the grace of God, I might be able to encourage or touch. To this day, that vision for my future ministry is as clear as if it happened yesterday.

I was being addressed by the great command in heaven. The headquarters of the Almighty was saying,

You are being placed in a battle position of world consequence. I'm trusting you with a message to be proclaimed from a strategic center that is looking out upon the Orient and the world. The going will be tough, but you volunteered for the voyage, and you promised you would be my servant.

Don't be afraid. You will not be able to handle it yourself, but I'm going to be with you, and I will do it through you. Simply believe and follow. If you allow me, I will enable you to touch nations and desolate towns to the ends of the earth.

I accepted the mandate with thanksgiving, asking God for help to fulfill it. I felt as if I was going into a battle of world consequence, with a strange mix of fear and faith. I didn't know *how* he would do it, yet I knew he would be there if I would let him.

In so many words the Lord was saying to me, *I prepared you for this mission before you were born, and throughout all these years I have been waiting until you were ready for the position and the position was ready for you. Now everything is finished. Now go ahead! I'll take care of all your future. Get on with it!*

That was my sendoff, and I came down from the mountains to Berkeley with a tremendous inner sense of promise. I didn't tell anybody about my Tahoe vision. I didn't want to tell anybody about it—it was too sacred. But I knew that God's hand was upon me.

Sobering Reality
While keenly aware of my limitations, I was confident that God would

lead me through. But I was not prepared for the deplorable situation that greeted me at the church. The church leaders had just agonized through two years of controversy. The pastor had fought the local governing body's efforts to remove him and then appealed to the Synod level of the denomination. After more than two years of this ecclesiastical infighting, the pastor finally left, leaving the congregation a confused, divided flock. When he left he took about a hundred members with him. Many of these were Sunday-school teachers and loyal followers, even a few pillars of the church.

My first appearance was on Rally Day Sunday. I found there were fewer than a hundred men, women and children, including the babies, in the whole of that Sunday-school hour. The only adult Bible class was a small group of mostly retired men who met together each Sunday morning. The week before, the junior and junior-high Sunday-school teachers had simply not shown up, choosing to go with the pastor as he organized a new congregation from his followers. Unfortunately, they left without mentioning their intentions to the superintendent or the children in their classes. The group moved two blocks away to the Women's City Club and set up their own worship service.

The shock of that first day at Sunday school was like diving into the icy waters of Lake Tahoe in early spring.

Attendance at worship was encouraging, though, thanks to the faithful remnant who came to hear their local boy returning as their pastor. Would I be able to handle this first delicate exposure? The conflict had dominated the local headlines for months. Every evangelical church in the Bay Area was aware of the struggle going on at First Church Berkeley. No doubt some of the four hundred who showed up that first Sunday were more curious than serious. They had to discover who we were and see if they wanted to be with us.

During the first eighteen months, we cleaned up the membership rolls, which hadn't been touched for years. During my second year we reported the removal of one thousand names from the church roll. The statistical loss of members affected the entire Synod. That record pleased no one in the denomination! But the cuts were essential, and everyone knew it. And it got even worse. Of the nineteen hundred names listed on the roll, only six hundred could be found who expressed a desire to remain active. Of these, only about three hundred displayed any real desire to participate in the work of the church. We were, however, blessed with the reappearance of many who came back to renew their relationship with us. I thank God for those special men and women who were willing to stay with the church, believing it was God's place for them. I will be forever grateful for those faithful, loving elders whose brave hearts welcomed my leadership with joy and wholehearted effort.

By the grace of God, from the start there was growth in both attendance and active faith. Over the course of the years, we filled first one service and then two, with some twenty-four hundred worshiping each Sunday morning. When I left there were three thousand members in the congregation. The turnover was always constant and rather rapid because so many younger families were moving out of the more expensive Berkeley community to newer homes in the suburbs, over the hill toward Walnut Creek. But this was not negative. It was positive, because we had the opportunity to train new people to fill the empty places of leadership, unlike those communities where leadership remains stable and changes are more difficult. Our start was fast in Berkeley because of the quality and faith of leadership among both the stalwart adults and the remarkably committed students.

Remarkable Student Leadership

During the war years, even though the congregation was not in a happy state, the student leaders of the college department, known as Calvin Club, remained loyal. Functioning independently, they produced their own program activities, conferences and social events at a high level of excellence. They knew they had something to offer their fellow students at the university—a warm, attractive Christian fellowship. During registration, they would go up and down the lines, hand out leaflets and encourage students to join them in their meetings, which were indeed well planned by the students themselves. All that was going on when I arrived. Shortly after I came to the church we started an evening service. Many of those students would be there, close to the front, with increasing numbers of young singles and some teenagers joining the growing group. (TV had not yet invaded the culture.)

Adults who loved the more informal service and the fellowship with youth also joined us. This was my favorite hour of the week. With a song leader, familiar hymns and gospel songs, the sermons were popular expositions of biblical truth of God in Christ. The evening services were informal enough for special features and presentations as well as for unplanned, spontaneous interchange and fun. The semicircular seating arrangement and balcony made possible a warmth and intimacy of fellowship not achievable in the more elongated, cathedral-like style of many sanctuaries. With a youthful congregation led by a college and youth choir, I felt free to speak their language and speak the truth of Scripture as I saw it.

Getting Across the Mandate

From the start, I endeavored to present Jesus Christ as the hope for the world. I wanted the congregation to know we were involved in the biggest and most important enterprise on earth. We were engaged in a spiritual conflict of greater significance than World War II. We were indeed to be the *shock troops* of heaven against Satan and his hosts. Indeed, Christianity was the greatest of adventures, making immense demands with limitless possibilities for good and for God. It had cosmic, eternal scope and exciting, everlasting rewards. To follow Christ fully called for dedication, just as war called for dedication and sacrifice.

To give our lives to Christ without reservation, we risked having our life strategies changed, often on the spot. Coming from the "boot camp" of my own experience of nine years in Hollywood with the young people of the war years, I could speak genuinely and earnestly of the price and sacrifice of dedication and commitment. Obviously, such concepts would not make sense to many perfunctory pew sitters, or even to those taking their first steps following Jesus Christ.

At one time Jesus told his disciples, "I have many things to say to you, but you cannot bear them now" (see Jn 16:12). Soon, however, there were those for whom these things *did* make sense and who were eager to receive them and live them out. Both cause and commitment moved more freely to the front in preaching and program. In Sunday-morning services where I was addressing a mixed multitude—often with critical student minds analyzing and questioning what they heard—my sermons were more along the themes of "taste and see that the Lord is good," while the evening service would often offer the challenge "forsake all and follow me."

A handful responded to Christ's call almost from the first hearing of the good news. For them, the Christian life became a way of excitement and fulfillment. As Jesus promised, in giving ourselves away to him, existence began to take on even greater meaning for many. They began to "have life and have it abundantly." It was as simple as that.

It was out of these informal evening services, where the sermon carried the implicit message of commitment, that "My Heart—Christ's Home" seemed to evolve spontaneously. I am not sure why this simple, artless sermon seems to speak so personally and deeply to people about the presence of Christ with them and in them. Of all the hundreds of sermons that I have preached through the years, none has had the life-changing impact and continuing influence of this one. Perhaps it has to do with people's hunger for a faith relationship with Christ and my sharing in the first person various aspects of my own spiritual journey.

A Postwar Miracle

I marvel now at the response to the gospel during the war and the postwar years, especially in my first years in Berkeley. God did more than I ever could have imagined. Definitely far beyond human capabilities. At the forefront was the dedication of veterans attending the university, quickly followed by young couples and single adults. Nothing was more moving than to see young men and women quietly trust God enough to give their lives to Christ in committed service both at home and overseas. None of this happened overnight, of course. It takes *intention and time* for God to grow mature Christian leadership capable of knowing his will for a life decision. But a remarkable number *did* make the decision, volunteered, went on to spiritual "boot camp" and "officer's training," were assigned to a ship under the flag of the cross and sailed the high seas with Christ their Captain, Friend and Savior.

During the summer of 1951, we ordained twelve young men for ministry into our denomination (PCUSA). As I write these words I hold before me a church bulletin from that year which lists the names of fifty-four men and women, including spouses, who were in seminaries, all preparing for Christian work at home and abroad. At one time, a few years later, we had nineteen missionaries from our church serving in the Middle East, embracing everything from the Sudan and Egypt to Palestine and Syria up to Iraq and Iran and reaching as far as Pakistan—all difficult fields of service. But that was the nature of the times. Youth were ready to endure difficulty, hardship, even danger for a great cause. They were challenged by the human need and the spiritual battle.

Contributing Conditions

History was preparing a canvas for us on which would be sketched the portraits of scores of these men and women who would volunteer to advance the cause of Christ wherever the need was greatest. Most of them are still on the battle lines, serving with distinction. For these recruits of the faith, the disciplines of serving and living out the gospel fit like a glove, and they were up to the challenge. They gave themselves to a battle they knew would count for time and eternity. The context of the day was forwarding the gospel with a mighty surge of spiritual energy, a paradox of anxiety and boundless confidence.

The old order was changing. It was an hour of death and birth—a *kairos* hour. The sovereignty of the Western world over the Third World was fast drawing to a close. Imperial dynasties were passing off the scene. Britain, France, Germany and other powers had been devastated and impoverished. Their roles of leadership no longer could be maintained. Astride the world now were two great powers, America and the Soviet Union, soon to be locked in contest with one another in a fearful expenditure of armaments and precipice diplomacy that would evolve into the Cold War. The nuclear age was upon us, and the antagonists began stockpiling weapons of mass extinction they hoped they would never have to use. The explosion of nuclear power had threatened the existence of humanity.

There was an awesome sense of the possibility of the end of the world in our time. By 1947 some members of our congregation were digging bomb shelters in their own yards to protect their children from what they feared would be a nuclear attack. President Robert Sproul of the University of California at Berkeley came back to the campus after a six-month leave of absence studying the conditions in Eastern Europe and the Soviet Union, and he solemnly said that within a year's time we might very well be living underground. He made that a public statement in the Greek Theater, as I sat there, realizing the sobriety of the moment.

A Prepared Public

The operative word in business and in our homes was *fear.* We, too, prepared for the worst by storing food and water so we could shelter people in the basement areas during a nuclear attack. The flip side of this individual and corporate fear was a bold, assertive United States—far more powerful than the Soviets, although we didn't know it at the time—that continued to flex its military and economic biceps at home and abroad. The United Nations was founded, bringing great promise alongside an equally great peril. It was a wild, new age of opportunity.

We all asked what could be developed for good through the nuclear discoveries and the application of nuclear power as a positive means of energy. The Scientific Age had come of age. But this time, it was more than a technological savior; it had also created the seeds of what could be total destruction.

It was a bipolar time: enormous despair vied with unbridled hope. As we saw and felt America's growing strength, our church recognized the increasing possibilities for witness. We remember General Douglas MacArthur issuing a call from Japan for missionaries, believing that this would be one of the means of reconstruction in Japan. This was the *kairos* hour, a time of danger and opportunity as hundreds of thousands of veterans returned to civilian life across the country, with tens of thousands crowding into our nation's campuses. UC-Berkeley was the recipient of some of the best and the brightest our country had to offer. What a tremendous challenge to the Christian community to meet and associate with these mature men and women, many of them tough and battle-hardened. For them, risk was a way of life. They had seen it all; they had put their lives on the line. There was no danger too great and no risk too frightening. Those who became followers of Jesus took that same never-say-die attitude and made the next courageous decision to give themselves to an even higher cause: to become warriors for Jesus Christ wherever God might lead them.

For these new soldiers of the faith, the disciplines of preaching and living out the gospel fit like a glove, and they were up to the challenge. They gave themselves to a battle they knew would count for time and eternity. The context of the day forwarded the gospel with a mighty surge of spiritual energy. We were witnessing a prepared public, and history was preparing the canvas on which the portraits of spiritual conquest would be drawn. Unfortunately, there was also a contingent of servicemen who saw the church as an opportunity to build structures and enjoy the social hours more than train and develop themselves for higher Christian service.

This bent for a life of ease, to the exclusion of commitment and sacrifice to Christ, spawned a mindset that for many affected how they raised their own children—the children of the sixties. A considerable number of the renowned "flower children" were children of these veterans who later gave themselves more to comfort, security, money and success than to a pursuit of life's higher values. The generation of the fifties was largely fed on sawdust and found itself reacting in the sixties to the new *I'm Number One* mentality. That's why I say it was a crisis hour.

A Prepared People with Prepared Leadership

It was into this exhilarating high-seas engagement that I came as a prepared pastor with a mandate. It was my joy to find an equally prepared people ready to go to work for the cause of the gospel. I found no entrenched resistance. I was not just welcomed; I was welcomed enthusiastically. Even with our reduced numbers and strength, we enjoyed the unity of the Spirit and the bond of God's peace. We were ready to move ahead and believe God was with us. The members of the church made a concerted effort to welcome others. We were becoming a "user-friendly" congregation. The steady growth in attendance aided the recovery of their joy in the Lord. It imparted confidence and made them eager to share with others what they were receiving. I shared with the people excitement and wonder and, at a deeper lever, the sovereign grace of God.

At the outset I was not sure how the people would receive me. I was a son of the church. My father and mother had been leaders there, and my mother, my sister and her family were still actively involved in the life of the congregation. I felt somehow that the congregation might still think of me only as a high-school youngster.

Instead, they embraced me as though I was coming home to my own family and heritage, which was true. The congregation felt I knew them and understood them. They saw me as one of their own kind. I spoke their language. They appreciated my more informal style of relationships and leadership. Instead of criticizing me as one of their own sons, as parents and congregations often do, the opposite occurred. They defended me and took pride in whatever their "hometown boy" could do. They were not only for me within the church but defensive about any criticism. Without such strong congregational support, I'm sure I would have felt more sharply the arrows of outside critics, questioning the way we conducted our youth conferences, our unapologetic emphasis on evangelism and, to them, our outlandish commitment to foreign missions. Having been humbled by the experiences of the immediate past, the church was now ready to embrace the good news that God was forgiving of their past resentments and criticisms and truly loved them. A fresh touch of his grace stirred their desire to share it.

There was an exceptional core of student leaders in our Calvin Club college department. Most of these were women, and leadership was a task that fell to them largely because during the war manpower had been drafted into the military. These strong, able women, some graduates, some still in school, kept the tradition of Calvin Club alive throughout the war as the largest Christian fellowship at the university. They maintained its strong evangelical witness with a high quality of fellowship and fun.

The elders of the church were a special gift of God. From the depths of my heart I thank the Lord for these earnest, able men, most of them twice my age, who trusted me and let God lead them on into new and daring steps of faith. Their affection, loyal support and quiet faith opened the door for God's Spirit to move and bless. Their positive attitudes quickly influenced others.

Spiritual Awakening Among Students

Immediately following the war, unusual spiritual awakenings startled several evangelical colleges and Bible schools, such as Wheaton, Asbury, Moody Bible Institute and others. In certain large assemblies a powerful sense of God's holy presence produced a deep conviction of sin, a brokenness of repentance, tears and utter submission to God, followed by forgiveness, cleansing, boldness of faith and fresh abandonment to the will of God.

Classes were suspended. Entire campuses were caught up in the movement of the Spirit as students, inwardly driven in agony to confess their sins, began to get right with God. Then they remained to pray and encourage others to experience their joy and deliverance. It was my privilege to see it happen at the Moody Bible Institute in February 1947. It came completely unexpectedly and unplanned. It was a work of the Holy Spirit in ways I had never seen before, nor have I seen since. It was a touch of the revivals I had read about in the eighteenth and nineteenth centuries. Its influence was felt by Christian students across the land, particularly evangelical ones, who would quickly pass on the news to others.

In July 1947, Henrietta Mears was holding her annual Sunday-school workers' conference at Forest Home, California, where one hundred or more Sunday-school teachers had come to be taught and inspired by her leadership. Henrietta had just returned from a trip through the razed areas of Europe.

One evening, she shared with the conferees the appalling suffering and destruction she had seen on her trip. She simply poured out her heart as she saw the saving power of Christ as the only hope of the world. It was a Spirit-enlightened message, stirring the hearers to the depths. After the meeting she gathered a few of her student assistants, summer interns, to pray with her in her cabin. Among them were Bill Bright, Lou Evans Jr., Dick Halverson, Bill Dunlop, Jack Frank and an equal number of young women. (Henrietta was ahead of her time in encouraging women to engage in important ministry roles.) As they continued in prayer, there was given a burden for a world racked in agony and despair.

Toward midnight they had a visitation of the Holy Spirit. There unfolded a vision of Christian students of America volunteering in a spiritual counteroffensive against the overwhelming forces of evil still dealing death, destruction and misery to millions in Europe and Asia after the holocaust of World War II. The vision included a mission. They were to begin a spiritual crusade to call Christian students to carry the banner of the cross where the need was greatest.

On into the early morning they talked and prayed, sensing they had been given an empowerment by God's Spirit to call the Christian youth of America to reach the non-Christian youth of the world. Their mission would be so to share Christ with the students they were able to reach that these in turn would spread out and touch their world with the gospel, which would create the possibility for lasting peace, sanity and salvation. They were to start immediately, and that they did. They renamed the coming conference, now calling it the College Briefing Conference, suggesting its almost military purpose of engaging in action for their cause. On her knees with the others, Dr. Mears saw a means of launching this new twentieth-century crusade.

Time was short. The conference was only six weeks away. There was no established network, no special funds. Some five hundred students were expected to attend, attracted by a call to sacrifice, to volunteer heart and soul to the cause of Christ. Believe me, God was in it. I, for one, bear witness as one participating in the preparation. But there was a supernatural power which seemed to spark and enable arrangements with electric communication and excitement. It seemed as though God himself was making all the complex arrangements, arousing interest in students and bringing all together, some not knowing why they had come.

The grapevine communicated that something was happening among Christian students. They crowded the conference all during the week far beyond capacity—possibly seven hundred in all. These were the seeds of a spiritual awakening. It was something God did without the planning of any particular church or small group. We could sense the Spirit of

God bending low over the earth, encouraging all of us to feel the same sense of expendability for the cause of Christ—the same earnestness that was hitting Christian campuses in other places. Students were beginning to see a spiritually starving world through the eyes of Christ. God was at work. His Spirit was blowing over manmade barriers, and those winds blew right into the ministry at Berkeley, filling out the sails billowing with the breeze of the Spirit.

This movement of God in the hearts of students added to my excitement and fueled my fire to fulfill the mandate given me as a pastor in a university environment. From the first, I had told the church my reason for being at Berkeley would be to present "the whole gospel to the whole world by the whole congregation," supported by Christ-honoring love and life. I took the mandate I had been given at Tahoe, and I reformulated it in line with the principles I had shared with the pastor-seeking committee and session at the time of my call. I share the list of these principles here as an encouragement to the reader, with the profound belief that they are as true and potent today as they were half a century ago.

Nine Guiding Principles

1. Our ministry was to be *centered in the person of Jesus Christ.* He is the source of our life, our Lord and our Savior, our triumphant and coming King. The heart of everything Christian is to trust God revealed in Jesus Christ, to trust Christ fully and follow him faithfully by the Holy Spirit who dwells in the heart of every believer and communicates his presence and provision. Christ is the center of all.

2. We agreed our ministry would be *supported by Scripture,* "the only infallible rule of faith and life." We were a Bible-believing congregation, fully aware of and obedient to the historical, exegetical studies of the Old and New Testaments. We were convinced that we held in our hands God's Word, the only infallible rule of faith and life, a trustworthy disclosure of God's ways with his creatures and a trustworthy record of the

way of salvation. Our job was to preach it, teach it, study it, trust it, obey it and assimilate it into every area of our lives.

3. We believed a fresh hands-on ministry was to be *led by the laity.* The men on the session whom I had inherited as the incoming pastor had executed their offices with ability and with all earnestness. They felt they were responsible for the welfare of God's people in that congregation, and they applied what they were learning in their secular responsibilities to their work within the church. They did what they were expected to do with the knowledge they had. It was a marvelous beginning with a quality of lay responsibility and leadership I had not seen in my previous congregations. I quickly learned I could trust them, so I encouraged them to carry on their various offices, praying that the Father would guide us and use us for his glory as he chose.

4. As a people we were to be *bonded in Christ's love,* looking to him to impart the love we needed to love one another even as he had loved us. We would ask him for the grace we would need in order to maintain a spirit of unity in the bond of peace, enjoying the wonder of his presence. At a future point, when the cry of spiritual loneliness was clearly heard, the dynamics of "life together" in the body of Christ moved to the front.

5. We would allow this mutual love of Christ and one another to *permeate our lives and motivate us for mission.* I knew that if there was to be any ultimate spiritual success within our congregation, it would be because of this deep, abiding commitment to care for others. We would be committed to an outreach to the entire world. Our church would look beyond itself to the needs and lostness of hearts and souls of people wherever they might be. We would serve Christ by representing him to the ends of the earth with the good news of the gospel. This, of course, was the special mandate I had been given at Tahoe. So my prayers and efforts moved in that direction. In various ways God held my feet to the fire until I was able to communicate to many in our congregation the enormous potential and privilege of world mission.

6. We agreed we would *care for the bodies as well as for the souls* of our neighbors. We would seek to love our neighbors as ourselves. I did not see this in the first years as clearly as I did during my last year at Berkeley and then in Seattle. Nevertheless, the awareness was there, and we would make the commitment to love our neighbors as ourselves, to touch and reach the whole person, body and soul.

7. We encouraged our people to *team together for maturity, mission and guidance.* My understanding of the nature and importance of teaming developed in the following years and became a major value for ministry while I was experiencing it in action during the 1970s at Fuller Seminary. I'm now convinced that teaming is essential to protect, direct and empower Christian leadership today. We would help each person as an important member of the team to fulfill God's commission for us. Yes, we were individuals. But we wanted to be more than that. We would be a *body*, strong, energized, committed to allowing the Spirit of God to lead us in ways impossible as isolated individuals. We were convinced that no one person could do the job of ministry or crosscultural mission alone. If anything of significance was to be accomplished, it would be done *together,* with Christ as the center.

8. We emphasized *the empowerment of the Holy Spirit through prayer.* This was the ministry of the congregation. From the outset this principle was practiced whenever an executive group, a committee or just a few people gathered for even the smallest function. It was understood that first we would recognize our needs and endeavor to place them before the Father and ask for his guidance, control and blessing.

If Jesus prayed all night before he called the twelve disciples to serve, if he prayed until sweat as great drops of blood fell to the ground as he wrestled through his commitment to the will of God on the cross, then to follow Christ in any degree of redemptive effectiveness meant we also must spend time in prayer. This is the truth most growing congregations know and practice, but in static or dwindling churches it is invariably ignored. To attempt to do supernatural business with merely natural abilities ultimately is futile. It simply does not work. We must take God seriously and be willing to let him operate the business as we pray and let him do his work in his way.

I believed him and endeavored with limited ability to make prayer primary both for myself and for others who were traveling with me in Christ. A favorite author of mine at the time was S. D. Gordon, who asserted that *prayer clears the field of battle; service merely occupies.* I believed him, and I endeavored to man my own artillery piece and encourage others to make prayer *primary* for spiritual action. It is my prayer that today's churches will become worshiping bodies of believers with a genuine heartfelt praise to God for all he is and all he does. In our current secular society, so barren of bright hope and so full of fears and anxieties, I would make worship, thanksgiving and an exaltation of the triune God the centerpiece of every aspect of congregational life.

9. We would *let God lift us above self and circumstance through worship and praise.* We would worship the Lord in thanksgiving. The words of the Thanksgiving hymn would prayerfully be on our lips:

We gather together to ask the Lord's blessing;
He chastens and hastens His will to make known;
The wicked oppressing now cease from distressing,
Sing praises to His name: He forgets not His own.

Beside us to guide us, our God with us joining,
Ordaining, maintaining His kingdom divine;
So from the beginning the fight we were winning:
Thou, Lord, wast at our side, all glory be Thine!

We all do extol thee, Thou Leader triumphant,
And pray that Thou still our Defender wilt be.
Let Thy congregation escape tribulation:
Thy name be ever praised! O Lord, make us free!

Pastor Jack Hayford has a booklet entitled "The Heart of Praise." In it he tells the story of how he began his ministry of the Church on the Way with only twenty members. They decided their primary purpose would be to praise God and make the service one of worship and exalting the Lord. That small band of believers wanted to lift up a testimony, simply pointing to the sovereign grace of God who triumphs over all things. Pastor Jack's church began on its knees, and that's the way it continues with its multiplied thousands today. The hymn "Majesty," which he wrote, reflects the key to any vibrant, relevant ministry. To worship his majesty attracts and builds the people of God, bringing love, joy and peace when offered from the heart.

I see this more clearly now than I did then, that *always* God's glory is worthy of my adoration. His mercy and grace evoke praise and rejoicing in his goodness. Together, God gives us an experience of divine reality. God's greatness and power and love are seen when "the things of earth grow strangely dim in the light of his glory and grace." A knowledge of who God is and what he has done for us opens the heart to a fresh flow of God's love, joy and peace with fresh faith and heart for obedient action.

These nine guidelines for the renewal and mission of the church and the spiritual development of the people pretty much summarize what I have learned through my years of ministry.

Applying the Principles

We were not a perfect people. Every church has its problems, and Berkeley was no exception. But even during times of stress and difficulty we were blessed with a surprising degree of unity. There was general agreement on who we were in Christ and what we were to be about. The pulpit, or course, was the natural rallying point for giving direction to the entire congregation.

Looking back and evaluating the spiritual development of our student leadership, I see that, without question, one of the most important things I did was to gather a few interested students to meet with me for fellowship and prayer at 4:30 on Saturday afternoons.

We asked each other how we were doing and how we could pray for each other. I would read a paragraph from Scripture, give a few comments and share my understanding of its value and meaning. Often I would read a few pages from the life of a Christian leader or great missionary to quicken their interest to follow in the pattern of the great, challenging leaders of the past. We would then talk about how we could we apply those proven principles in our own situation on campus or with Calvin Club leadership.

I would also share with them my needs as a pastor. I felt I could be more honest and open with these young men than I could with the congregation in general, because I knew that they were with me in a common commitment. We recognized that some of our overenthusiastic evangelistic efforts were less than effective, and we discarded them in the interest of being more responsible and effective. But these were all lessons important to the understanding of the complexities and opportunities of being a Christian in a secular society.

Without being fully aware of what was happening or of the importance of those hours together, we saw a large number of the students who offered themselves as expendables for Christ anywhere in the world come out of that fellowship. With the growth of the congregation and the delegation of responsibilities to others, the composition of the congregation moved toward people of mature age, but the Saturday-afternoon pattern continued with the younger ones. For me, those Saturdays were treasured as a high point of close fellowship in Christ, bonding us together in his love and praying together in the power of the Holy Spirit. Only later did I figure out that the most effective thing God had given me to do was to motivate and develop Christian leadership for world service. From that group came the influential pace-setters for world ministry and mission mentioned earlier in this chapter.

Keeping Spiritually Fit

As the ministry developed in Berkeley and became more complicated with increasing size and multiplied programs, my daily hour of devotional Bible reading and prayer was not adequate to keep me in close touch with God. I found it necessary to put in my calendar *stated times* when I would be alone with him. About once a month I would drive up to a remote spot high in the hills above the university, only a matter of minutes away. The teeming cities of Oakland, San Jose and San Francisco were spread out before me, and I could see the Golden Gate which headed to the ends of the earth.

In that setting I would remain alone for the morning and sometimes into the afternoon, seeking a fresh word from God through Scripture, prayer and the Holy Spirit. Given my diabetes, fasting was not practical. Then with multiplied responsibilities came innumerable interruptions, emergencies and demands, further complicated by conferences, outside appointments, speaking engagements and denominational boards on the national level making their demands. Soon a monthly extended appointment with God was scheduled in my date book as seriously as a blood transfusion for one with leukemia. It was my means of restoring my soul, of correcting my course and my conduct, assuring me of his covenant promises and the task remaining for me to do. To this day, for me, time alone with God—both daily and protracted—is absolutely essential.

Pastor's Home Base

I wish now that I had been more aware of my primary ministry to my family. Why did I not see this at the time? When I began my ministry, it was expected of a pastor to put the church above himself and the family. I see so clearly now that the family should have *priority* for any pastor, not only for spouse and children but for himself.

When I married Edie, she was secretary to Dr. Stewart MacLennan, minister of the large First Presbyterian Church of Hollywood, whose

Sunday-evening radio expositions were heard up and down the Pacific coast. So she knew what she was getting into! A loving companion, a marvelous hostess, a gifted manager, she quickly showed me I could trust her to take care of all our household affairs. After a lifetime together, I feel even more fully that she is the one person in all the world for me!

Edie was still an undergraduate. College women, knowing she was a student on their campus with them and sensing her interest and understanding, were attracted to her. They clustered about her on Saturday mornings in our home to talk over their concerns, problems and feelings about themselves.

Edie soon reached out for further professional training to be of more help to them and others. After completing the half-finished bachelor's degree in English literature that she had started before we were married, she went on to receive a master's degree in counseling psychology. During my next charge, in Seattle, she completed another master's, in social work, at the University of Washington. While I was at Fuller Theological Seminary, she fulfilled a long-time dream by earning a Ph.D. in clinical psychology, and since then she has been practicing as a clinical psychologist while giving me support in my ministry.

In all of this she gave priority to our children, Marilyn and Monica, and made sure she was always at home when they returned from school. She participated in the life of the congregation, involving herself as she had time along with her roles as mother, wife, student and spouse of the pastor. I marvel at how she was able to keep her priorities and put it all together so ably while she pursued her profession as a psychologist.

Edie, our girls and I continued to enjoy August together at our vacation home in the Santa Cruz Mountains at Mount Hermon. The girls say that they really got to know me as a father through the stories I would tell them as I put them to bed every night and through our hours at the beach in the afternoons, the associations with a few friends with children of the same age as ours, and just relishing our time together. Those were joyful weeks for me and a happy time for them. The only problem, Edie would say, was that I was always so wiped out by weariness the first week of our vacation that I would simply drop out of all family participation. Obviously I was overstretched.

The Growing Organism

For vibrant health, any organism needs appropriate exercise as well as good food and drink. The same is true for the spiritual growth and strength of a congregation and for individual Christians. Exercise is vital: doing things for others, loving, caring and serving in the name of Christ. The primary service we were seeking to render to others during those years was to share the good news about Jesus Christ—both with those near at hand, through evangelism, and with those at a distance, through world mission. Not until I had learned the hard lessons of the sixties did I become aware of the equal importance of loving the neighbor who is right beside us, through a concern for civil rights and social justice.

Efforts in Evangelism

In the exercise of evangelism, the situation was different in Berkeley from that of South Hollywood, primarily because we were now in an academic community where students and university graduates were disciplined in learning to think for themselves. They were told *not* to make commitments until they had thoroughly investigated or thought through whatever the appeal for action might be. Therefore, to give an invitation at the end of the sermon and expect people to be ready for a response was not helpful.

Earl Palmer, in recent years, and in the same situation in Berkeley, has made it clear that his evangelism was first to *expose* the hearer, student or reader to Jesus Christ himself as we find him in the New Testament: to help the person understand who Jesus is, what he has said and what he has done, and thus to build confidence in his trustworthiness.

That was also my approach, although not as well articulated. I too desired to help people get to know enough about Jesus to be willing to experiment, to know more, to venture, to take a step forward, even simply to begin to pray for light. Then, as they would follow the first flicker in obedience, more light would illumine their way. Faith grows one step at a time until there is strength enough to make the large commitment of trusting oneself wholly to Christ. First, we trust him for his forgiveness, acknowledging him as our personal Savior; then, in love, we surrender all to him for his control and direction. Though it all happens in a moment of crisis for some individuals, for most of us it is a process.

I learned early in my ministry that authentic steps of faith in Jesus Christ seldom come about through a Sunday-morning worship service. The significant work was accomplished in the small groups, the summer conferences, the fellowship times and the personal conversations. I endeavored to point a person to Jesus Christ, help him or her understand who Jesus is, then invite the person to venture at least a short step of faith—to follow him in the light that was already available so that more light might be given. If I gave an invitation, it would not be to come forward to make a decision for Christ. It would be, "We have further information if you desire some help in getting to know God personally in Jesus Christ." I would then encourage them to come forward. An elder or one of the staff would talk to them either personally or in a small group. We wanted them to ask questions; we were eager to find out where they were in their lives, and we endeavored to respond appropriately to their point of need.

I inaugurated a class on Wednesday nights at 9:00, after the midweek service, on the credibility of Christianity. It was limited to those who were not believers. People were not allowed to join that group if they already were a member of the fellowship or a convinced Christian. They could bring a friend, however, and stay just one time with their acquaintance. We usually would have ten or fifteen in attendance each week.

Joining me in leading the group was one sharp senior student who could answer the students' questions better than I could. Between the two of us we managed quite well. I encourage any pastor or youth leader to take the risk of starting such a class. It will keep you sharp, and your vulnerability will help make you a more effective communicator and servant.

Looking back, I remember two spectacular examples of how God worked in people's lives through that class. One young man was an avowed believer in communist doctrine and a foremost critic of Christianity; nevertheless, he continued to search for more and more truth. We challenged him to read the original sources of Christianity before making a judgment about any person or movement. Before long, the Gospels got hold of him and so stirred him that he found it interfered with his job as a printer of fine art. He took a day off and drove his car to a quiet place, determined to decide for or against the gospel. His decision turned his life around and led him to graduate study in England and then service in Mexico with the Quaker "Friends" organization.

The first night of the class I had invited Dr. Thaddeus Hoyt Ames, a Christian psychiatrist from New York City. We developed a close relationship while he was in Berkeley, and out of that friendship came a rare human experience. I invited him to come to our group as an exception to the rule, because he wanted to know what was going on and to observe it. I knew I could count on him to handle questions from students who often were more emotional than rational in their arguments. Early in the session one hostile student challenged me by asking, "Do you believe in hell?" After a momentary pause, Dr. Ames turned to the student and with a surprised look on his face said, "You mean you *don't?*" That turned the tables around, putting the young man on the defensive. His reasons for denial were not very convincing even to himself. After the rest of us left that evening, Dr. Ames counseled with the young man. His hostility against God arose from the pain of a father who had deserted his family without even a farewell. Dr. Ames taught me much that evening, especially not to be fearful of those who are angry at God.

My own knowledge of Christ came from a derelict cry at sea: "Lord, help me; show me the light that I may walk in it." That became the formula of my own gospel presentation. First, pray for light that God himself will help you know who he is. Allow him to go to work on the inside with your own thinking and feeling, ask him to reveal himself to you, and then go on with him from there. I found this more productive than endeavoring to reason and rationalize truth with my own intellectual limitations. Also it had been my own experience. I had cried out in the darkness at sea. I did want light. A month later it was given. Both the cry and the answer were real. Reality communicates.

Here's a key point that sums up my entire Berkeley experience: *The faith of students and the congregation grew more by walking in the light than by sometimes impulsive and radical decisions.* The decision times were at our conferences, where we had opportunity to enjoy warm, close fellowship—where decisions could be made in the close community of love. Dr. Dick Halverson, later chaplain to the United States Senate, has a great paper titled "Community as the Context of Evangelism," in which he says the best evangelism is done with the support of loving friends in a fellowship of believers. Only when we're free to ask questions and to have some light cast upon our intellectual problems can there be the kind of faith that will be supported later. If we move on the basis of our feelings alone, without satisfying our intellectual reservations, our decisions will tend to be short-lived and unsatisfactory. God wants to have us know the truth, to understand, and to put our faith in Jesus Christ, the Way, the Truth and the Life.

Six Approaches to Evangelism

Bill Hybels, pastor of Willow Creek Community Church in Illinois, writes about "stereotyping evangelism" in his bestseller *Honest to God.*

Bill gives six categories for evangelism that are appropriate at some times for some people but are not appropriate at all times for all people. Perhaps from this short list which I have paraphrased you will discover how God may use you most effectively in sharing your faith. Evangelism can be

1. Confrontational. We all know that some people will come to Christ only if they are *knocked over the head* and confronted with someone like a brash Peter. Fortunately, God has equipped certain believers with a combination of personality, gifts and desires that makes it natural for them to confront others. If this is your gift, use it as an appropriately aggressive salesperson for Christ.

2. Intellectual. Though he could be confrontational like Peter, the apostle Paul often used an intellectual approach to evangelism. What about you? Are you comfortable giving "reasons for the hope that is within you"?

3. Testimonial. The blind beggar who had been healed by Jesus had only a few words in response: "One thing I do know: I was blind, but now I see." Many seekers of truth don't need to hear a sermon. All they need is a solid, sane, normal Christian to share with them, "Here's what God has done to change my life."

4. Relational. Some people are effective communicators right where they are, loved and trusted by others. Uncomfortable talking with strangers about matters of faith, they are able to share freely with friends and colleagues. These people may not be good knocking on doors and passing out tracts, but they *should be encouraged to cultivate their regular contacts through prayerful purpose and intention, seeking opportunities to share the good news.*

5. Invitational. This is the "come and hear" evangelist. If you are bashful or afraid to go toe-to-toe with individuals in assertive evangelism, *ask them to come and hear* a message, to enjoy a holiday service, a concert or a play on a Christian theme. This is one of the most overlooked forms of evangelism today. If this is your style of sharing

Jesus, then you might say, "My goal is to fill a row of pews."

6. *Serving.* One of the most endearing people in Scripture is a woman named Dorcas. She probably never knocked on a door or preached a sermon, but she did something wonderful: *through her acts of service she pointed people to her God, who could transform human hearts and fill them with love* (Acts 9). If you are one who feels most comfortable serving, you are among the most valued of evangelists.

There are many ways to let the light of God shine through us. The important thing is to love people around us enough to make an effort, using the ways which we find comfortable and satisfying and venturing out in faith.

The Korean War—Threat of Nuclear Destruction

While we were on vacation at Mount Hermon in August 1950, the Korean War broke out. It seemed to us at that time that we might be involved in a nuclear holocaust. In due course China got into the fight, with Russia's nonbelligerent support, changing the entire war scenario. In those early months of the war there was almost universal anxiety that this could indeed trigger a nuclear engagement. The first week of that vacation I had been reading the two-volume work on the life of J. Hudson Taylor written by Mrs. Howard Taylor. I was immersed in thoughts of world mission. But when news of hostilities hit, ultimate issues became immediately relevant. I prayed, *Lord, what should we do? In two or three months we may have a nuclear holocaust, with San Francisco a probable nuclear target. What should the role of the Berkeley church be?* I wrestled with these questions. First of all, I knew that those of us in Christ were secure. I believed that to die and be with Christ promised to be far better than the present. Edie, the girls and I were everlastingly safe. I knew I did not need to worry about the future of my own family. But the family of the people of God, the larger community of faith at the church, was a concern to me. What about them? What if we have only a matter of months before there is an obliteration of the whole Bay Area? Earnestly I interceded. "Lord, what would you have me do? What priority should I give in these next months? It's most important that I know."

After three or four mornings knocking on the door of heaven, I became frustrated when there was no clear answer. Then I sensed, prompted by the Spirit of God I trust, that he was saying, *Munger, why are you asking me this question? You know very well what my will is. I told it to you in the Great Commission and at the end of all four of the Gospels. If that were not enough, I've given you the entire book of Acts to explain how important it is to be witnesses, first at Jerusalem and then to the ends of the world. You know already what to do. Now do it. Just do it.*

My reply was, "But Lord, how is that possible? We have pressing financial needs to operate the local church program. Can we function effectively and still devote energy to missionary emphasis?"

God brought me up short. *Do you not think I'm able to do it for you? Now trust me and simply do what I say.*

The Venture of Obedience

After further prayer, I resolved that when I got back to Berkeley I would present the session with the suggestion that we challenge the people to give to world mission as they were led. At that time we used the duplex envelope system where people could give both to current operations of the church and to benevolences or missions. I consulted with a few of the leaders of the session and then risked recommending to the board that we take our hands off and let God's people give as the Spirit led them. We would trust the Lord to supply our local need.

The first person to come to me upon my return was my associate, the Reverend Bill Antablin. Early in our conversation, before I had mentioned my experience, he said, "Bob, you know Florence and I have been much in prayer about the will of God for us. We've been here now going on four years, and we have prayerfully thought it all through. We feel our place is on the mission field. We have applied to our board of mission in New York, and they have accepted our application. We now plan, at the conclusion of this school year in June, to proceed in an appointment to Lebanon, where my parents were born. We both feel this is God's place for us."

Wow! So there it was. Bill was committed before I had even shared with him what had happened to me. It sealed and empowered our confidence that God was in this new step. It was an order that came directly from above: *Get going further on the mandate!*

We shared our mutual confirmation of God's plan with the staff, and they quickly got on board with us. All this happened within a matter of days of my return. That jolted the session, because they felt their responsibility to care for the funds entrusted to them. The proposal was taken under advisement until the next month. At that next meeting, a humble man with a heart for God rose to his feet—Mr. Ralph Pettis. I can still see him standing before us, twirling his spectacles in his right hand. With unusual conviction, he gave a final word after the long debate. "Brothers," he said, "we have been talking about the importance of mission all the time I've been in this congregation, and yet we've never had enough courage to put our action where our mouth is. We've never given the people an opportunity to do the will of God as they choose. Don't we really trust them? Don't we really trust God?" Nothing more needed to be said.

Within three or four years the benevolence giving by choice of the donors built up, with fifty percent for world mission and the other fifty percent for local needs. To the amazement of some, but not all, of us, the local work also flourished. Every year God miraculously seemed to respond. In due course, during the last three years, we were also in a building program. Then the offerings were divided into thirds: equal amounts for local benevolences, world mission and the new building. Yet the amount for world mission continually increased. God so blessed that when I left for Seattle, we were paying for the building and still continuing to handle the other two 50-50. It was a marvelous demonstration of how God supplies the means when we are about his will. When we trust him enough to sacrifice, the lesson is simply "trust and obey."

The term "faith giving" was current. We understood it to mean venturing beyond estimated income so that God would have an opportunity to supply our needs supernaturally and thus increase our faith. That's what 2 Corinthians 9:8 was all about. For some, it seemed a bold, revolutionary method of trusting God. But it worked. Somehow funds came in to enable us to meet our commitments. It was an exciting time. Numbers of us learned that the second tithe is easier than the first. As a result of this emphasis, I believe the congregation was an encouragement to other churches for obedient trust in God to carry out his own work.

An Expanding Vision

In 1954 God was good to give Edie and me another, closer and more comprehensive look at a world in need. Bishop Jacob of the Church of South India invited me to hold a six-week mission in his diocese in Kerala. Our priority contacts were missionaries from our own congregation and denomination. The intention was to extend a word of greeting and encouragement, then return with a firsthand report. Naturally, we took advantage of every opportunity to learn more and visit Christian enterprises and individuals about whom we had heard. There is no better way to see a country than through the eyes and heart of veteran missionaries. We stopped in Korea, Taiwan, Hong Kong, Thailand and North India. The most exciting ministry was in Kerala, with an interpreter and faithful servant who traveled with us and took good care of us. We went from industrial cities to hill people, and from jungle villages to educational centers, staying for three or four days in each location. We attended the vast Maramon Convention of the Mar Thoma Church, where forty thousand Christians sat on mats on the sand of the dry river bed under a *pundle* (roof of palm branches) and heard E. Stanley Jones and others.

The exposure issued in an unexpected insight to the primary contribution our congregation could make to the missionary cause. More important than numbers of missionaries or adequate funds to forward the cause of the gospel was the sending of mature, discipled servants of the gospel—the kind of people able to communicate their faith, establish churches and reproduce others committed to Christ. What impressed me was the impact those from our Berkeley church had been making in Asia and the Middle East. Both the recent ones, whom I knew personally, and the veterans sent out under Dr. Lapsley McAfee, who was pastor thirty years before, stood head and shoulders above the others, it seemed to me, in quality of Christian leadership and productivity. In our American churches there are thousands of earnest, dedicated pastors, but not all are visibly bearing much fruit. It was the same on the mission field. Sending people overseas or to a spot of spiritual need does not guarantee they will be productive and see the results in changed lives.

So we wanted to do a better job in preparing people to be effective, spiritually productive servants of Christ. The Billy Graham San Francisco Crusade of 1957 offered a marvelous boost and encouragement. Over three hundred of our members were trained in personal evangelism for use as counselors in the crusade, which lasted for six weeks at the San Francisco Cow Palace. Experiencing the benefit of the training one night a week for four weeks, they wanted to learn more about how to be effective in sharing their faith and being prepared to meet their opportunities. Many were ready to give time and effort to that purpose. That led to a regular Wednesday-evening curriculum at the church called "Encounter with Revolution," with a variety of staff-led classes incorporating principles from the Nine Guidelines. This was experimental and tentative but gave evidence that God's people were ready and willing to be active followers of their Lord—obviously not everyone in the congregation, but the representative few who chose to venture the journey of faith in earnest.

Spiritual Warfare—Faith Tested

The postwar years in Berkeley were not a smooth succession of uncontested spiritual victories. Quite the contrary. I found myself engaged in a conflict of cosmic dimensions, with the powers of truth fighting those of falsehood, light vs. darkness, the kingdom of God vs. the forces of evil, Christ and his followers vs. Satan and the demonic host. Since that time I have learned more about spiritual warfare, but much of it was a mystery to me at the time.

There were remarkable breakthroughs of faith and new life, countered by savage counterattacks of the enemy—each event part of an ever-developing plan we could not grasp. Elements of revival in the historic pattern of Wesley and Finney seemed to be all around us. With a small group of student leaders, we prayed for renewal of faith and life—for our congregation to have a true spiritual awakening. We believed renewal was possible and near at hand. This was strengthened as we heard news of the Holy Spirit interrupting classes during a five-day mission to students at the Moody Bible Institute in which long lines waited patiently to make public confession of their sins and seek restoration with God, in brokenness crying out to God for mercy and pleading for power to live a godly life. And we heard that God was doing it in greater measure at Asbury and Wheaton colleges. "Why not at Berkeley?" we prayed.

Spiritual Battle at Forest Home

The second wave of attack came during the summer of 1948 at our Forest Home College Briefing Conference. The students had been studying Navigator materials when tension began to develop between those who were "into the disciplines" and those who were not. Those who were regularly studying the Bible, memorizing Scripture and praying were tempted to think of themselves as spiritual giants. At least that was the way some of the more intellectual students viewed them. Others desired a more intellectual support for their faith, more rational, less experiential.

At that second college briefing conference, Dick Halverson challenged students to join "the fellowship of the burning heart," asking students to agree to spend an hour a day in Bible study and prayer. Our group returned to Berkeley with some division. Two or three of our promising future leaders quietly backed away. A more balanced, understanding approach would have kept them growing and contributing their gifts to the Calvin Club fellowship. I felt responsible in a very real sense. I should have taken their feelings more seriously, given special time to them, listened to their complaints and sought God's answer to their problems. It is a lesson I have not forgotten.

During that same Forest Home conference, I came down with Type I diabetes. As I was flown to a Bay Area hospital for observation, the experience itself became an unusual testing of my own faith, because during the conference I had offered myself as "an expendable" to God. The decision had come at a crisis time in the conference when the destiny of six hundred students seemed to be at stake.

But was I willing to be expendable?

In the hospital my own doctor's anxiety and apprehension didn't help. I was uncomfortable with the way he handled me. He seemed to be frightened and confused, not knowing how to treat me. He was so fearful that his concern also filtered through to one of the nurses, whom I thought I heard say to her replacement, "He is terminal." After that, the nurses seemed to be treating me with special concern. I knew little about diabetes except that my father's close associate had died of it a few years before. After a long night and day of struggle, by the grace of God, finally I could say, "Lord, the sharpest pain will be leaving Edie and the girls, but your will be done." And his peace was imparted. It was my second encounter with death.

Once again I found the Lord trustworthy. The adjustment to a rigid diet and insulin injections drained me of time and energy when I seemed to need it most. But the covenant was still in force, the mandate still held; God was faithfully fulfilling his promises, diabetes or not. The Forest Home conference ended in a glorious victory for

God in hundreds of young lives.

That was my baptism into spiritual warfare. The attacks had not ceased, but my confidence in the power of God had grown. He is able to meet and master them. So I entered the fall of 1948 at a low point physically. Spiritually I had been thrown off balance, disoriented, unable to take advantage of the many usual means of renewal, such as energy for protracted prayer. Paradoxically and wonderfully, God was quietly at work that very year gathering many incoming students whom he would lead into ministries at home and abroad. Spiritually, it may have been the most productive year in my ministry.

I want to say a word about the testing of my faith during those days. For one thing, it was never easy. With every new opportunity came new challenges, but always with new victories appearing in the course of time. In the first years particularly, 1947-1951, we were engaged in intense spiritual warfare. There were elements of great spiritual advance, but we had also opened ourselves for counterattack by the enemy. I was praying positively for the advance of the gospel. I prayed not only that God would show us renewal in the local congregation but also that he would give us the *pattern of renewal* that he had given his people in the past.

I was praying for advance, but I was not praying defensively. I was not praying the Lord's Prayer. *Lead us not into testing, but deliver us from the enemy, from the evil one*—I had not prayed that way. As a result, I was wide open to attack from the enemy, and so was the church. Then it was that I learned to pray *defensively*.

I was now fifty years old. Where could I best serve God in my remaining years? Was there another strategic situation where I could be used to encourage "world Christians" for service? I felt my mandate in Berkeley was concluding. I did not want to stay too long and have the church enter into a stage of decline. In the providence of God he gave me a new challenge. Without this fresh mandate and refreshing infusion of power I would not have had the ability to meet the developing crisis that made Berkeley front-page news across the land.

7
Community:
Weathering
Crosscurrents

TRUE SUBMISSION NEVER DIMINISHES

TRUE PERSONHOOD. IT IS NOT A PASSIVE,

MINDLESS RESPONSE TO WHATEVER IS SAID,

BUT A CONSCIOUS CHOICE

OF A WILLFUL SURRENDER TO DIVINE LOVE.

Jack Hayford, *Taking Hold of Tomorrow*

For me, the years 1960-1962 were a loosening of the sense of *mandated direction.* I began to feel that I had done about as much as I could in Berkeley; I didn't have any further strong sense of responsibility or commitment. The facilities were under way, the mission program was maintaining the same high level of giving, and the financing of the new educational building was reasonably secure. If there was ever to be a time to make a move to another congregation, this would be it.

In the winter of 1960 I was flying over Panama after an overseas mission in South America when it suddenly came to me clearly and distinctly. I was struck with the awareness that there were only two spots in the whole world that I felt would be of comparable challenge to me after the great experiences I had enjoyed in Berkeley. Number one would be the Evangelical Union Church in São Paulo, Brazil. It was one of the most unusually well-attended Union churches in the world. It had a strong evangelical emphasis, and it occurred to me that a ministry there would open an opportunity for me to begin to work with American personnel. They, in turn, would begin to bear their witness and perhaps disciple Christians in the secular fields of their own calling. The other great possibility would be the University Presbyterian Church in Seattle, pastored by my old teammate at Princeton, David Cowie. I knew Dave was having some thoughts about returning to Southern California.

Storm Clouds

I discovered the church in São Paulo had called another man and was well under way with its new pastor, so that door was closed. That left Seattle. Within a year David Cowie resigned, accepting a call in Southern California.

I felt it was time for me to move on and, in fact, had a certain fear I had perhaps already stayed too long. I had seen this happen with some of my colleagues in ministry. It would have been easy just to hang on without any strong sense of commission or mission, but I sensed storm clouds were looming ominously over the Berkeley horizon and in other parts of the country, because of the escalating awareness and reality of social injustice, racial problems and other glaring challenges facing American society at large. I knew trouble lay ahead. Would I be able to shift from our strong emphasis on mission overseas to give more attention to the immediate issue of our neighbors?

I was becoming aware of what now, in current language, is called the *cultural mandate*. I thought often of how we were given a mandate at the very beginning of time, when God introduced the first pair. Adam and Eve were told both to cultivate the Garden and to express the will of God in their relationships with one another and with nature. With mounting ecological problems, the social challenges and other issues that were coming to the fore, I knew we would have to respond to that twofold responsibility.

I also sensed there would soon be no peace in Berkeley.

In that changing social context, did I have the spiritual strength and God-given dedication to lead the church, maintain our commitment to overseas missions—and at the same time enthusiastically lead the congregation into understanding the more sensitive political issues which the social causes presented? If I chose to captain the ship around those rocks and shoals, I knew it would be tough. Perhaps that is why I felt I would rather leave Berkeley while everything was harmonious and at a high level of unity than face the inevitable conflict that might well cause trouble for my closest associates and trusted leaders.

The Struggle

I prayed about what to do, trying to get God's guidance, but I received no real spiritual mandate. In the times of extreme stress that would come later in Seattle, I often wondered whether I had really listened to God or whether I had simply taken the easy way out of the challenges of Berkeley, particularly when the church there was forced to confront so many crises after I left. Berkeley graciously offered me a sabbatical, but if I had accepted it—I certainly needed it—that would have closed the door to Seattle. Still, all things considered, I knew Seattle would be the one place where I might be able to serve the Lord with my background of experience in a university community.

The Seattle church had an ideal location. Just as Berkeley had been a block or so away from the University of California campus, University Presbyterian Church was located within one block of the University of Washington. It was a church with a citywide influence. Berkeley was essentially a suburban community—a suburb of San Francisco, a part of the Bay Area mosaic. Seattle was a unity, and University Church was certainly the most influential in the city. Moreover, it had first-class facilities and equipment. I knew I would be greeted with a recently built sanctuary,

COMMUNITY: WEATHERING CROSSCURRENTS

in many ways one of the newest and finest in the city. The church also had quality parishioners and a marvelous evangelical heritage.

It seemed so logical that Edie and I should make the move to the Northwest. The people were genuine, though more conservative both socially and politically than their counterparts in California. The church also had civic leadership of importance. Arthur Langley, a member of the church, had been in the renewal movement of the city of Seattle and had been its mayor for two terms. He later served a full term as U.S. senator. He was an earnest Christian, committed to the Lord and of great influence in the city and the church. The church was also a flagship mainline church among denominational churches. There were so many reasons why the Seattle congregation offered unlimited opportunity for ministry.

And so, when the pastoral search committee contacted me and told me I was their top choice, I did not hesitate. We packed up and moved to Seattle.

The weekly attendance was about two thousand in the two morning services. (During the latter part of the sixties, when student alienation was peaking, we still maintained the attendance and the membership actually increased.) The Sunday-morning service was televised, broadening the church's visibility and ministry. Pollsters estimated that approximately seventy-five thousand people viewed the services each week, the majority of whom were not Presbyterians or even Protestants. There were large numbers of Catholics, Jews and nonchurch people who apparently were asking, "What goes on inside a Protestant church on Sunday morning?" They saw what was going on at the large, public Billy Graham crusades and on the programs produced by highly specialized radio and TV evangelists. But what happens in an ordinary Protestant service?

Lonely at the Top

As I settled in at University Church, I discovered many exciting doors beginning to open for me as the leader of one of the strongest churches in the nation. I was thrust out of suburban and into civic ministry at a time of major civil unrest and widespread social change. My position as pastor put me on center stage both nationally and locally.

However, I was without the network of spiritual encouragement and fellowship I had enjoyed in California. I also found it difficult to get close to many of my fellow pastors. Many were reticent about sharing their own lives with me. I know how they felt, because that's how I had felt in South Hollywood early in my ministry, with so many large churches surrounding me. Although there were the inevitable problems, looking back, I experienced the Seattle congregation as composed of gracious, loving, concerned, supportive and patient people—perhaps more patient than I.

Sudden Social, Cultural and Spiritual Changes

Although I had seen signs of social unrest coming, it broke with an intensity of force for which I was not fully prepared. I had much to learn about the issues and how to handle them. The sixties were rough weather for all traditional institutions—governmental, religious and educational.

More serious than this element of unrest was the students' rejection of the values and traditions of their parents and of the past. I will not attempt an analysis of the causes of this phenomenon. There are many reasons for it, but I think one could build quite a solid case that the benign neglect and permissiveness of some parents during the fifties were a contributing factor. Parents were busy finding their own future in their business and work. It had been a great time for prosperity and opportunity, for the building of homes and the establishment of communities. The postwar economy was booming, and people were prospering. But the children were often being neglected, and the values of their parents—material values—were fast losing their appeal. Swiss psychologist Paul Tournier said that while the parents were gaining in affluence and security, the children were finding that *possessions alone* often led to a life without meaning or value. Children often suffered from a lack of time and love rather than a lack of money. They were given money, education and an overabundance of comfort, but they were left with little of the legacy of meaning and purpose for living. Tournier deduced that because of their inner rage, youth began to turn against their parents.

The "Lost" Generation

Though I had experience working with the Berkeley School Board of Education on surrounding social challenges, I was surprised by the rapidity of change and the force of these even greater social upheavals in Seattle. You can imagine how the much more conservative people of the Northwest felt when the student change hit them.

The issues confronting us came in waves: racial discrimination, Martin Luther King Jr.'s marches, open-housing issues, the intensity of resistance and the growing awareness of the injustices in both the racial and social situations. To that was added the trauma of the war in Vietnam, including student concern with the draft and its implications.

Widespread social unrest was filling up our plates, and it was giving us collective indigestion. The alienation of truly thoughtful, discerning young people came to a crescendo with the assassination of President John Kennedy, his brother Bobby and then Martin Luther King Jr. The effect of these tumultuous events upon the students was so traumatic that some have called the student population of the sixties "the Lost Generation." But perhaps they were more *left* than *lost.* Left to their own devices without a moral rudder to guide them into the rough waters of social change.

Now that the generation that preceded them, and the strong, assertive leadership that has dominated the evangelical Christian movement since the war, is now reaching retirement age, we are forced to ask the question: *Who will stand in the leadership gap as we move into the twenty-first century?* The question is, does the second generation, which should now be in prime leadership positions, have either the quality of conviction or the gifts of leadership that the previous generation held? Leighton Ford, in much of his writing, encourages those who *are* leaders today to become aware of what is lacking and to do what they can to help develop strong, new leadership for the next generation.

Souls and Justice

My concern in this book is to move even farther down to the *fourth* generation, to those potential leaders who are now in their late twenties and early thirties. We must give these men and women the training and mentoring they need so they will be able to develop their full maturity and strength. This new generation must know that Christianity is—and always *has* been—two-legged. It must walk on both feet: with love for people's souls and with a burning concern for people's rights and privileges. We need to love our neighbors—and we need to care for them as Christ cares.

Without justice, people cannot feel Christian love. An African-American pastor once said to me, "You white Christians say that you love us black people, but how can I accept your love when you are standing on my feet and when you are stomping on my toes?" Those words hurt then, and they hurt now, because they continue to be true on all levels of the social structure today, just as they were for me as I began my ministry in Seattle.

A Severe Test of My Navigational Competence

Though not as large a church (there were three thousand members in Berkeley and four thousand in Seattle), Berkeley was united in purpose and mission. The Seattle congregation, with its multiplied programs and its diversity of viewpoints, was not nearly as unified a fellowship. I now realize I could have worked harder the first few years simply to win the confidence of the congregation and not pushed so fast and hard to accomplish my own agenda. I could have been more patient, loving and supportive. I could have listened more intently and wisely to people—staff included—before I began to tell them what *my* vision was.

The key lesson I learned in Seattle was this: *People do not follow their leaders until they learn to trust them.* I was a different personality from my predecessor. I was more reserved and depended a great deal more on the individual initiative of the leaders and session officers. I just said, "Here's an idea—let's look at it together." Instead, I could have been asking "Where are you on this?" and "What do you feel you need?" before I began to give them what *I* felt they needed. My spiritual 20/20 vision is so much better these many years later. Perhaps you have the same challenge in your life.

The demanding weekly television ministry, radio, preaching, teaching and administrative duties all kept coming at me full force in this new setting. At times, I felt I was drowning in an ocean of people, much as I had felt so overwhelmed by the tempestuous seas those many years ago. But I did not take the challenge personally. All pastors were in trouble, I would argue with myself. All leaders were experiencing the same tensions. All Christian leaders, in a sense, were seeing the church support everywhere beginning to fade because of the multiple problems in society. Nobody could win 100 percent support, I reckoned. I was a great analyzer. Strong left brain. Not so good at taking personal responsibility for what was happening all around me.

Unexpected Challenges

I wish I could convince all those thinking of Christian leadership of the importance of this key truth: *The church is more than a believing organization; it is a spiritual organism. Its life, vitality and purpose are fulfilled through personal relationships.*

Indeed! It is the body of Christ. Every true believer is "in Christ" and is designed to function as a member of his body, intimately relating to him, the Head, and to other Christians as fellow members.

Consider how our bodies function. All members, such as the hand or foot, are related to the head and respond to impulses generated from the brain. But the impulse travels from the head through the arm to the hand by innumerable connections. There's an upper arm and there's a lower arm. Bone is joined to bone and served by attached tendon. In turn, the tendons are connected to muscles, and the muscles are fed by vessels conveying warm blood from the one beating heart. The complex system is controlled by a connection of nerve endings which instantly obey the directions of the head, telling the hand and fingers and arm and the rest of the body to make the desired moves. Every member and every function are mutually supported and helped by all the others. A member is helpless without fellow members and body connections.

In a spiritual sense, the body is quickened with life received through Christ by new birth through faith. Growth comes through *feeding* on the Word of God (Mt 4:4), and strength is produced by *doing* the will of God (Acts 5:22) and *rejoicing* in the grace and love of God (Eph 5:20). The body also needs personal food and nourishment. We can't get along without it. The blood purifies the body and provides a cleansing effect to carry away the impurities from the cells and vessels.

So the blood of Jesus Christ also imparts strength to the body of believers and provides for ongoing purification. In like manner, as body members we need to confess our sins to one another to experience the full cleansing of the Spirit of God.

German theologian Dietrich Bonhoeffer makes this clear when he says we need to have some significant person who is there with us to affirm us and give us the assurance of absolution, to remind us that we can indeed go in peace, knowing we are forgiven by God. Is this the inner spirit at work? Yes, but that same body needs the outer words of a significant, trusted Christian brother or sister.

In Seattle I came to see the building of relationships and the full development of these "body life" principles as my primary learning experiences. A new situation with urgent needs calls for new approaches. I am told it takes miles of slow circling to change the direction of a huge tanker or battleship. It cannot respond to the helm quickly, due to its tremendous weight and size. Similarly, a large congregation does not turn around, change its attitudes and respond to new leadership easily or quickly.

That is why, when leadership is delegated and shared, it is essential that the pastor and his associates agree and cooperate on purpose, priorities and program. In Berkeley, the new staff person would need to adjust to a well-established direction and to me as the senior pastor. In Seattle I was the newcomer, and I wasn't fully aware of the importance of making an effort to understand people's feelings, their convictions and their attitudes toward my goals and objectives. I had carefully reviewed the guidelines with the search committee and session, and I felt, with God's help, that we would be a good match.

I found time together with the other pastors on staff and our program directors to be an invaluable way of building deep-level personal and spiritual relationships. We met Tuesday mornings for two hours and continued after lunch for another hour. I also endeavored to meet for thirty minutes each week with the staff members, giving them an opportunity to share what was on their own mind and hearts. I wanted the staff to tell me how I could best support them. I'd never felt administrative work was my strength, but this was one way for me to use my abilities to serve as a bridge to bring the staff together in mind and heart. That association with my staff was indeed a congregational lifesaver during the many crucial moments of the tempestuous sixties.

The Cry for Relationships

In spite of the excellence of our music, the creativity of our programs and the comfortable new facilities, many of the newer members drifted out of touch with the church. The lost lambs needed to be found, then folded into a close-knit, loving relationship to be fed and nurtured, as church-growth studies make clear. However, our church lacked a good system of enfolding and integrating new believers into the life of the congregation.

What was true for the newer members was also a need in the hearts of the old-timers. They, too, needed encouragement and opportunities to renew their relationships with one another, to share what was happening to them and to go deeper in their relationship with God. We needed one another. Though they would see each other in formal worship and in numerous church activities, there was neither the openness nor the honesty of close, trusting relationships which could allow people to warm each other's lives with the love of God. A turning point in my own understanding of this subject occurred through reading Bonhoeffer's *Life Together*. The application of the last two chapters of this seminal book became basic in my endeavor to achieve open, honest, forgiving, cleansing relationships in the body of Christ.

At the same time I was discovering the openness of relationship in Scripture. There was no tape recorder in the wilderness at the time of Jesus' temptation, so he must have shared with the disciples how he had been tested by the enemy, by the devil himself, for forty days and forty nights. And again, going into the garden of Gethsemane before the cross, he spoke out in great anguish when he cried, "Father, let this cup pass from me," as tears overcame him. Jesus knew and allowed others to know his inner suffering and pain even as he communicated his deepest feelings with the Father. His words from the cross echoed for all to hear as he unashamedly cried, "My God, my God, why hast thou forsaken me?"

So I took a risk and began to venture into this more vulnerable, open style in my preaching and teaching, and later in small groups. Almost immediately I began to experience its liberating, cleansing power.

A Pastor Shares His Struggles

I am convinced everybody is carrying burdens, hurts and frustrations. Even the most exuberant and seemingly secure, satisfied individual may be covering inner pain, distress, even the torment of guilt. So when the preacher does not seem to evidence these human experiences and let others know he has failures of his own—even discouragements and doubts—he or she is not being fully honest. The strongest witness Christians can give to the reality of Jesus Christ comes when they disclose to nonbelievers that they too are struggling to stay above water in the circumstances and trials of life. At the same time, believers can give witness to the amazing love of a God who forgives them and is with them in the struggle, offering strength and help.

In my own preaching toward the end of the Seattle period, I was beginning to let people know that I was with them in the struggle and needed their prayers and help just as they needed the Lord and one another. That principle was further verified later in the faith renewal teams at Fuller Seminary, where this relational approach became the vehicle through which personal testimony was presented in various congregations with honest, real, long-lasting effect.

One of the basic lessons on the unity of the leadership of the church is that *the fellowship of believers must have honest, candid, vulnerable one-on-one relationships.* We began by designing constructive approaches that brought unity to the body of the session during the time of extreme social crisis. This was especially effective when we were confronted with radical, secular students—even our own young people—who were espousing extreme ideas on sex and social issues that rapidly brought division between the two segments of the church: youth on one side, adults on the other.

Some Encouraging Responses

Even though my own personal enthusiasm may have been premature and even misunderstood, I knew there was a deep need for personal relationships with Christ and with each other as we encountered great opportunities to fulfill the Great Commission. Before long, the emphasis upon small groups made an immense contribution to the spiritual growth of our congregation. We started rather slowly with this program, because we knew that, for some, being vulnerable to peers would be difficult, if not painful. Prayer and prayer groups had always been the focal point of my own ministry, from the days of Forest Home and the indelible influence of Henrietta Mears. I knew praying and sharing were essential for ministry, and I always endeavored to make them a part of my personal and church life. But the atmosphere of the sixties was creating such a different social backdrop that, for some reason, praying at this level of intimacy was becoming increasingly difficult for me. There was also some resistance to the small-group approach, because there had been certain abuses of small home-centered prayer meetings led by people with ideas contrary to the direction of the former pastor. Those experiences had engendered considerable distrust of prayer groups in general.

In the second year we established "Know and Grow" groups. To know Christ and to grow in him, we said, it was necessary to know each other and to grow in our relationships with each other. In the course of time, the Faith at Work approach was a great help to us, giving us the insights we were looking for. The human potential movement, current in the secular field, was also widely emphasized in our small groups. However, these sessions on occasion would go too far in their endeavor to strip people of their defenses. Always a danger—both then and today. But we did emphasize sharing. We asked questions such as "How are you doing? Where are you hurting? How can we help you? What have you learned this week in your walk with God? What would you like to know in order to be more effective in your walk with him?" This was all bathed in honest, from-the-heart prayer for one another.

During the last years of my ministry in Seattle, we were all blessed with the presence of Roberta Hestenes, who joined our staff to help us emphasize interpersonal relationships with the Scriptures as the central force. This sensitive, brilliant woman developed an effective ministry of neighborhood Bible studies which became a solid outreach to the neighbors of our church members. Leaders were developed in Roberta's own inductive Bible study groups and then challenged to join with at least one other member, after which the two of them would invite neighbors to examine the primary sources of information about Jesus Christ. So many were interested in Jesus, but few knew much about him. So members of these small groups would simply say something like, "Suppose the two of us meet together once a week to take a look at the Gospel of Mark [or whatever book they were studying] and see who this person Jesus really is and why so many feel he is God." Soon the leadership would be passed on with proper materials to one of the new people, so that the method could be shared not just by one person but by all in the group.

This was not a fellowship group, but a Bible study designed to arrest and deepen the interest of non-Christians who were friends of members of the church and eager to know more about the claims of Christ. From day one, Roberta's leadership made this program a great success. In time there were dozens of small groups meeting at homes or in the church. God blessed that ministry in ways none of us could have predicted.

During my last year in Seattle, I ventured an early-morning group with graduate students and recent grads from the university, to discuss in advance the subjects of my sermons. I invited the students to come and give their feedback on a passage of Scripture or a book of the Bible on which I was going to be preaching in the coming weeks. For example, I would take the book of Romans and ask the students, "If you were teaching this, how would you make it relevant to people today right here in Seattle? What does it mean to you, and how can it be applied to your own personal situation?"

It was a great experience for all of us. These students gave me a wealth of information and insights on how and what to preach. Before long, this weekly fellowship developed into a special support group in which these future leaders could share for personal prayer and counsel in areas where they were struggling with their Christian faith.

Every Believer a Potential Leader

All these "relational" experiences focused my attention on what became another basic lesson about ministry that I learned in Seattle: *Every true believer must be seen as a potential leader for Jesus Christ. Every member of the church should be seen as a potentially positive, mature, effective influence.* Today every effort should be made by pastors to provide each man and woman with opportunity, encouragement and support in their growth, so they may be motivated to recognize and exercise their spiritual gifts.

For me, the breakthrough of this radical truth became a compelling certainty through my experience as teacher of the trainees in the Bethel adult Bible-training class. In 1965, I became aware of the need to provide a deeper biblical understanding for most of the congregation. I was led to take two weeks to go back to Madison, Wisconsin, to prepare myself to teach the Bethel Bible Series.

When I returned, I found the recruiting technique really worked. I was surprised when twenty-five adults committed to a program of four years in which they might well be involved with three modules each year: one fall, one winter, one spring, each seven weeks in duration. The commitment was so demanding that each teacher had to be highly motivated in his or her desire to teach the course. Perhaps it was my lack of faith, but I never dreamed that ordinary members of the church would have the motivation to give Bethel that kind of time and commitment. I found we often underestimate the eagerness and the ability of the average layperson to be available to serve the Lord. That was my first great discovery.

My second discovery was the enormous inherent ability of many of our members to develop significant leadership skills. The most prominent of these individuals certainly was Roberta Hestenes, who now has a worldwide reputation in the field of Christian formation and discipleship. Roberta came to me after one of our services in which I had presented the call for congregational members to become teachers in the Bethel series. She asked me whether women were permitted to teach the Bible classes. I said yes, and I referred her to an article on women in the life of the church which satisfied her that she, as a woman, could be trusted to teach adult men. That settled the matter. Interesting in today's context, isn't it?

Roberta was in the class no more than a month when I recognized that here was a woman who had more ability to teach and to grapple with biblical truth than I had. She was endowed with a most amazing, gifted heart and mind.

Roberta went from being a busy housewife with three little children to part-time and later full-time staff member. After earning a master's degree in communications from the University of Washington, she was called to Fuller Seminary to become one of the most creative Christian leaders not only at Fuller but across the nation. Along with her academic duties she continues to be master of the small-group method to encourage Christian nurture and maturity. She eventually went on to become president of Eastern College in Pennsylvania. She is also chairperson of World Vision's overseas department and continues to be at the heart of the small-group movement and evangelical leadership.

Shining Possibilities

When I eventually left Seattle for Fuller Seminary, it was with a strong desire to pursue the practical teaching of small-group dynamics and to train pastors to train laypersons as gifted, able men and women equipped for Christian service.

Again and again I recalled my early Christian roots as I sensed God's leading in a new direction. I especially remembered how Henrietta Mears would gather those hundreds of young people around her as she taught us, prayed with us and encouraged us. Henrietta fully expected that we would all *respond* and become *effective servants of God.* She viewed every one of us as shining possibilities. She believed in us. She had no doubt that with God's help we would have an effective ministry and mission. The supreme delights of her life were first to see young people come to know Jesus Christ as their Savior, Lord and eternal friend, and then to see these *living possibilities* present themselves to Jesus Christ and allow him to lead them on into his will and ministry. She gave further encouragement by reminding us that with our gifts and abilities we would be able to influence an entire world for Christ. Since that was her vision, she imparted this keen desire in her followers. To Henrietta Mears I owe a lifetime of honor, love and respect. Who knows what my perspective might have become had we not been brought together during those early years?

When, after seven and a half years at University Church, I realized it was time to move away from the Seattle ministry and carry what I could contribute toward the next generation of pastors being trained at Fuller, it was only natural that my fervent desire would be to help deepen the spiritual life of students. I now knew from experience that a solid spiritual development would stabilize their personal connection to Christ. I wanted to encourage them to maintain that relationship with the Father through *koinōnia*—a sharing, caring fellowship and praying with others. They might be "professionals" in the strictest sense of one day hoping to become pastors, missionaries and church leaders. But in reality I would help them know that there is really *no* professional when it comes to being an alive, vibrant witness for Jesus Christ.

A Disturbing Question

We need to be reminded that Jesus began a lay movement. He himself was a carpenter. There was not a priest or Levite among the twelve disciples. There were a few professionals in the early church, such as the apostle Paul, but the cutting edge of church growth and leadership for the most part was carried out by the laity. Even slaves became bishops. Today, a similar pattern is emerging among Third World churches, where growth is so expansive there is no time for institutions to develop years of training. Of course we need education and professional competence. But we also need church members *who have been taken seriously by their pastors*—laypersons who are so thoroughly committed, motivated and instructed in the Word of God and his ways of ministry that they are able to cover all the bases of Christian service, both within the congregation and in communicating Christ outside the church.

The fact that so many pastors find themselves overworked, depressed, serving declining congregations, expected to perform a nonstop series of spiritual and administrative ministries all alone should in itself cause us to be aware that we have missed a basic biblical truth. Jesus gave *time* to develop his followers and lead them on into discipleship and ministry. The apostle Paul devoted his attention to his Timothys and Silases. His letters remind us how seriously he took all the members of the churches in his charge. If that is how this movement we now call Christianity began, why not make a special effort to recapture that first-century example and once again make our churches models for lay ministry and lay leadership?

Sunlight Floods the Seattle Ministry

During my last year in Seattle I saw a bumper sticker: "If God is not close to you, who has moved?"

Initially, even though I did not feel I had a strong mandate for ministry in Seattle, I did sense God close to me by his grace. But when it came to the freedom of the Spirit, to seeing God actively at work answering prayer and doing his mighty works, I felt some distance from the Father. It came to me that *I had moved,* not God.

In February 1967 an opportunity presented itself for me to have an hour with the great Christian leader John Stott, of Great Britain. We were both addressing a pastors' conference at Mount Hermon. We had become acquainted some years before when he had preached for us in Berkeley. Now I had an opportunity to be with him. I simply shared with him frankly the tension I was feeling in Seattle and the feelings of my own failure to rise fully to the challenge of the ministry there.

He had a few questions and then listened some more until I had told my story. He then said, "Bob, let's pray." His prayer underlined the simple biblical truth that through the cross of Jesus Christ, *he who confesses his sin is forgiven.* He reminded me that it is the gift of faith in the grace and mercy of God's love, carried fully through by the offering of Christ himself, that makes us clean and whole. A genuine peace settled down on my heart. Whatever might be the future, I knew God had heard. I returned from that conference to face new opportunities in Seattle as they presented themselves, with a confidence that God was, as he had always been, with me and for me. He was still my light, and I was still simply to walk in that light.

Since then I have often reflected on the distance between God and me. Was it my eagerness to have the Seattle church? Was it my overconfidence in accepting the call with neither a mandate nor a clear, certain assurance that God would carry me through? That may have been part of it. Or was it a degree of theological drift? Perhaps. I confess that my years of close association with the academic community and its critical judgment of the supernatural had made me less confident in proclaiming boldly and emphatically the biblical view of God's salvation for humankind. Perhaps I had even trimmed the frightening truth that the lost are truly lost. A degree of reticence had hindered me from being as forthright in declaring the truth as the years went by. Was it the loss of the network of spiritual support I had enjoyed for so long in California? Or was it just plain burnout, having carried a major ministry without a sabbatical break?

Although the student problems and the radical social and political tensions of the militant sixties increased during my last two years in Seattle, I was experiencing a closer sense of confidence that God was ultimately in charge of everything and would work things out for his glory. In the life of the congregation, growing numbers of Bible studies, deepening relationships with Christ and one another, and the coming of Dick Langford as senior associate—with Roberta Hestenes ably handling Bethel—were strong evidences of God's presence and power in the midst of the intensity of the tensions in social and political matters. We felt the ferment of students against authority and all institutional traditions, which became a constant strong concern, yet in God's grace we found resolution.

By the time David Hubbard talked with me about teaching at Fuller Theological Seminary, I would be free to accept. My assignment in Seattle had been completed. Despite the weaknesses, both the church and I had grown and prospered—by God's grace.

Upon leaving Seattle, I felt the storms had been weathered, the ship was in good hands, and the future held great promise for University Presbyterian Church. Under Dr. Langford's leadership there followed a period of rest, restoration and the building of a remarkable ministerial team. His successor, Bruce Larson, ushered in an outburst of spiritual vitality, with an amazing number of members of all ages participating in various forms of ministry both within the congregation and to the world outside. A nonprofessional ministry developed there before our very eyes. In subsequent days God has done more within that congregation than I could have ever asked or thought. I thank him for the faithfulness of those who gave me such great encouragement during the difficult sixties.

Now, older and hopefully wiser, but for sure ever on the grow, Edie and I would head south to Pasadena and back to our spiritual roots in Southern California. Another layer of the onion had been peeled away, and, with more confidence than ever, I knew God was in control. I would now be privileged to participate in a "life together" with my new friends and colleagues at Fuller Seminary, the subject of chapter eight.

8
Teaming:
Putting It
All Together

WE KEEP FORGETTING THAT WE ARE

BEING SENT OUT TWO BY TWO.

WE CANNOT BRING GOOD NEWS ON OUR OWN.

WE ARE CALLED TO PROCLAIM THE GOSPEL

TOGETHER, IN COMMUNITY.

Henri J. M. Nouwen, *In the Name of Jesus*

I was concluding a mission at Wheaton College when David Hubbard's secretary, Inez Smith, called me from California. She said the Fuller Seminary president was returning to Pasadena by way of Seattle and would like to accompany me on the flight back home from Chicago.

I was delighted to have this time with one of God's choice servants and leaders in the evangelical community. I figured Dr. Hubbard must have had in mind some promotional assignment for me, which I would have done gladly. Although I was on the board of trustees at Princeton at the time, representing the seminary alumni, I was always interested in the work of Fuller Seminary and its growing influence in this country and around the world.

On the trip back to Seattle, Dr. Hubbard was gracious and, as always, a good friend. As we talked, he reached into his briefcase and took out a ten-year "Forward Plan" for the seminary—a thick book filled with page after page of dreams and visions for the future of Fuller.

I was eager to know about the direction of the school, but I thought all the detail Dr. Hubbard was sharing with me a bit strange. As we approached Seattle, he said, "If I were to recommend your name to the search committee for a new faculty person in the field of evangelism, would you pray about it?"

His words almost jolted me out of my seat. My mind was all awhirl. *Of course, I'd pray about it.* But I also had a few anxieties, the first being my lack of academic qualifications to hold a faculty position in such a prestigious school. How could I teach at Fuller with only a master's degree in theology? Ph.D.s were a prerequisite to work in academia, Christian *or* secular, and I doubted my ability to teach classes at the graduate level.

But my anxiety didn't end there. I did not even consider myself an effective evangelist, which could pose quite a problem to *teaching* evangelism in a graduate school such as Fuller. I did endeavor to point people to Christ and counted it a privilege whenever I could lead a person to the quality of commitment that engaged and produced new life, but I never felt very comfortable in that role. I had to be honest with myself and with Dr. Hubbard: I did not feel qualified for the kind of confrontive evangelism that carries the initiative all the way through. Still another anxiety was whether I would have the potential to teach evangelism at any level, to say nothing of a graduate program. Would anything I might teach make students eager to share the Lord? That was my real question.

But while these many anxieties lingered, a tiny ray of encouragement also came over my spirit, because I did have the *desire* to be of help to those entering into ministry or who wanted to serve Christ either at home or abroad. I had picked up that concern in the early years when I worked so closely with Henrietta Mears in Hollywood and at Forest Home. Other great influences were my friends David Cowie, Clyde

Kennedy and the other fellows on our weekend deputation team back
at Princeton. And of course there was Dawson Trotman who would
always remind me, "Hey, Bob, just put your hand into developing men
and women for the cause of Christ." So simple. So direct. So profoundly
right! Then there had been the positive experience at Berkeley, where
the seminary students who had gone out from that fellowship had made
such a lasting impact on lives throughout the country and around the
world. There was also my current ministry in Seattle, where God was
blessing our church's outreach in so many ways. All of these things told
me that evangelism was indeed a primary personal desire of mine,
something I had always regarded as a high privilege, however ineffective
my efforts might be.

In the Throes of a Decision

While still casting Dr. Hubbard's invitation in my mind, a few of my
anxieties began to abate as I began to realize I truly did have something
to share with theological seminaries. I had been critical of their ways,
throwing rocks over the wall for too long. Seldom did I produce any
viable solutions to what I saw were endemic problems. Now, it seemed
God was saying to me, *Munger, it's time for you to take a more positive
role. Quit trying to create change from the outside. Now is the time to
get on the inside and be of some influence—in the right spot—regarding
your many concerns.*

It was a word from the Lord that I needed to hear. I certainly had
learned something of value during my last years in Seattle that would
be of help on the *inside* of theological education. For years I had been
aware of a lack of staying power, zeal and enthusiasm—not only in
pastors but in seminarians at large. In the sixties, an article in a Christian
journal, entitled "Emancipation of the Ministry," expressed what I had
often seen happening. I had been saying to myself, *These well-meaning
young seminarians need to know what they're getting into.* Now I felt
I would be able to help articulate those challenges from my personal

experience of thirty years as a pastor.

I had gone through the personal isolation of the pastorate, and I knew I could talk about unspeakable joy in the midst of pain with the authority of one who had been there. I could also envision an entire course on the various kinds of callings to the ministry. Each time I had been called, the experience had been different. Students needed to know there is no uniformity in the calling of God or the guidance of God. On the contrary, he deals with us as unique personalities and always takes into account where we are in our spiritual journey.

With this opportunity to go to Fuller before me, I earnestly sought the opinion of several significant people in my life, among them Bruce Larson and Ralph Osborne of Faith at Work. I also needed to know the feelings of my staff at University Church. I knew my leaving would affect them, and I wanted to be sure I got their honest opinion. With that desire in mind I asked my staff to join me away from the church for a short retreat, where we would have two nights and nearly three days in the home of one of our members, on the beach on the north shore of Puget Sound.

The last night together, we worked out some of the interpersonal problems of the church as best we could. Then I told my staff I might be going to Fuller. The last thing I said to them that night is as clear as if I were to say it today. I said, "When we get together tomorrow morning, we're not just going to discuss this initiative and then make a move. At eleven a.m. tomorrow I want to go around the circle and ask you to tell me honestly whether you favor my move to Fuller or not. I also want you to tell me why or why not."

The next morning I went around the circle and encouraged each person to ask questions and raise issues of concern to them. What would be best for them, for the school and for the church?

One by one, every staff person said it was his or her personal conviction that Edie and I should take advantage of this opportunity!

There came over me a marvelous sense of freedom. I knew my departure would involve painful changes for them, but I felt their unanimity placed a seal on my decision. That kind of decision-making process blessed them and told them that they were important not only to God but to me. At the outset of our conversation I had felt unsettled, not knowing what their response might be. But as we worked through our feelings together, our love and appreciation for one another grew. That is what community is all about. One of the great tragedies in so many of our so-called Christian fellowships is that such mutually uplifting conversations as these are so few and far between.

Decision Made!

Professor and author Robert Clinton says that after you go through a period of training in ministry, you mature in ministry. Only then will you mature in spirituality. That's where you grow in your knowledge of God and the leadership in God. You can be mature in knowing *how to minister* and still not be mature in knowing the *ways of God* in ministry. Those are important distinctions. Some have one without the other and vice versa.

When I made my decision to take the assignment at Fuller, I realized God had already brought me to a place in my life where he had given me a balance. I had gone through some difficult times in Seattle which resulted in my constantly growing in my walk with the Lord and my experience as a pastor. Now, putting most of my doubts, anxieties and fears aside, I was ready to share my honest experiences with others who one day would be taking my place in the church universal. I was ready to unload some cargo, and God told me this was the right time and the right place. Just *thinking* about a future ministry at Fuller took a huge weight off my shoulders.

A "Frantic Learner"

I arrived at Fuller and began my assignment. I was pleased the administration trusted me with the classes I was given to teach. It was a rewarding experience to find myself not a stranger on the faculty but considered an instructor. For the first time in longer than I could remember I didn't have to worry about sermons or staff problems. I had the luxury of focusing all my attention on my classes and my students. It was a remarkable learning and growing experience to be able to enjoy a physical, intellectual and spiritual renewal.

As part of my desire to understand the motivation of the young men and women I was teaching, I always had them sketch out two or three pages about their reasons for coming to Fuller. Amazing stories always surfaced. Increasing numbers of students each quarter declared their allegiance to Jesus Christ and to a wide interest in evangelism and sharing the good news with the world. Year after year those students contributed so much to me through the vitality of their own faith and the dedication of their lives. I expected them to do their best, and they, in turn, challenged me to do my best as well.

My own academic course work pushed me to be on top of my subject, although I admit at times I was only one or two weeks ahead of some of the eager young minds who sat in front of me day after day. I became what Max DePree, in *Leadership Jazz,* calls a "frantic learner." With my formal ministerial duties now at an end, I could identify with the feelings of the children of Israel as they finally came out of the wilderness into a land flowing with milk and honey. Seattle hadn't necessarily been Egypt, and Pasadena was no Israel, but for all practical purposes they might as well have been.

The Challenge of Servant Leadership

Whether in our seminaries or in our congregations, vast numbers of teachers, pastors and students become inheritors of a tradition but lack a personal relationship with God. In their quest for academic glory or ego-driven pulpit appearances, some have desensitized themselves to the presence, power and purpose of the living Christ. Anticipating the future needs of my students, I witnessed many who were orthodox in their faith—they believed Christ truly to be their Savior and Lord—but who lacked the strong motivation, concern and commitment to impart new life to others through the gospel. Still other students would receive a call to share the message of Christ but seemed forever committed to struggling with how to integrate their belief with the rest of their lives.

This was where I had found myself during my own seminary years. I believed; I had received a divine call; I knew that Jesus was my Savior and Lord. Still, so often I struggled in vain to reproduce that quality of life which would be of honor to the Father.

Then there was yet another group of scholars at Fuller who were called and already eminently equipped to share and serve in the power of the Holy Spirit from the very start of their seminary work. There had not been many of those individuals in my personal seminary experience. But now Fuller would give me the opportunity to be of help to any and all these groups of young men and women, regardless of who they were or where they happened to be in their Christian walk.

The Joys of Being a Servant

It was once generally assumed by graduate schools of theology that seminary students had already matured in the faith and, therefore, that the institution was absolved of any responsibility to lead them further in developing and nurturing their spiritual lives. Today—and even when I was at Fuller—the key issues of Christian formation and discipleship are being taken much more seriously. Little did I know that after all my years of seemingly endless formation, I would *still* have much to learn as teacher and student. I learned so much from the students in my own classes and still regard them as personal treasures.

I especially find myself reflecting deeply on my courses on intercession, where at the close of class three or four students would always gather in groups to share, pray and support one another. Those men and women were not on campus simply to achieve academic excellence, as important as that would be to them in their future ministries. The real reason they had come to Fuller was to be sensitized by God, energized by the Holy Spirit to do his will and to use the words of World Vision founder Bob Pierce: "Let my heart be broken with the things that break the heart of God." They were learning to become servants as it was taught and modeled by Jesus, Paul, Epaphroditus, Timothy and other Bible stalwarts. I, too, was learning the fine art of servant leadership, alongside them each step of the way.

Every time I think of a "faithful servant" I think of our servant Matthew, who was so close to us in our brief overseas mission in the Indian state of Kerala in 1956. True servanthood is marvelous, and Edie and I saw it embodied in Matthew, who was assigned to travel with us as we moved from village to village. Every night he positioned himself for sleep on a mat in our doorway. As soon as we were in bed, he would put his mat down at the entrance of our room and would stay there until daylight. He would then get up and be about his daily chores. We felt secure and safe because we knew Matthew was always there to look after us. He was our servant, attending to our every need. That kind of dedicated, always-there servant is what Paul was talking about when he referred to himself as a bondslave to Jesus Christ. My friend Matthew was often in my mind at Fuller, as I made discovery after discovery on the powerful, life-changing influence of servant leadership.

Leading from Behind . . . Lifting from Below

Another surprising discovery for me was that one can motivate others from the rear position of leadership even better than from the front. I was not pulling my students toward spiritual things as an "up-front" leader; I was, in fact, providing direction from behind. I was pointing to Christ, our life, our leader and our Lord. John 8:12 was my theme then, as it continues to be my guide today: "I am the Light of the world. So if you follow me, you won't be stumbling through the darkness, for living light will flood your path" (LB). By coaching, teaching, modeling, encouraging, instructing and sharing, I was leading from the rear—*and lifting from beneath.* My ministry of instruction, counseling each student as an individual and in small groups and giving simple, consistent affirmation, was a new experience for me. But it was the only thing that made any sense. It's simply the biblical Barnabas role of paying attention to the spiritual development of others by encouraging them and letting them take first place.

In all this I was neither reticent to share my struggles nor hesitant to admit I was failing to be the full servant and model Christ wanted me to be. Besides, I don't think I ever could have faked it. My students would have seen through me immediately, had I tried any games or subterfuge. I simply struggled to keep my commitment to being a servant leader and hoped the spirit of my decision would be caught by the students. One of our themes was "The Son of Man did not come to be served, but to serve, and to give his life as a ransom for many" (Mk 10:45). We learned that the light of Christ shines from *any* location, above or below. Wherever he is allowed to be known and when his will is done, *his light shines.* (The fact that students caught this truth was certainly not due to my academic prowess, because I had none.)

Fresh Movement of the Spirit
In the spring of 1970, the anti-Vietnam War fever began to reach a crescendo in our universities. The Kent State tragedy exploded across our headlines and television screens. With our own eyes we saw the National Guard mow down American students on their own campus. Immediately those became the "shots heard 'round the world," especially the student world. By demonstrating on campuses and shouting in the streets, through boisterous threatening and posturing, students who were against all violence were, in effect, creating the kinds of conflicts the very war they were protesting was engaged in.

The alienation was real. Students were disillusioned. The impact of the killings at Kent State was profound. I felt it at Fuller. I also felt it at Princeton Seminary, where I was attending a meeting of the seminary trustees. Some twenty-five of us were shut up for three hours our last day by antiwar seminary students who wouldn't let us out to catch our trains and planes home. Yet with anger, pain and angst descending on us at every turn, we began to see a student renewal movement slowly break out across the country—not only on university and high-school campuses but in the military as well.

During the next four years, we noticed a renewed interest among young people who were committing themselves to prepare for Christian ministry. The previous generation of seminarians often had come to study theology because they wanted more faith. Now came a crowd of students who came because they *had* faith—and conviction. They wanted to use their faith and share it, not just to add to it. There was a fresh breeze of the Spirit as earnest young men and women made evangelism the core of their spiritual lives. Sharing their new life in Christ was at the forefront of their desire.

This commitment to take the good news to the ends of the earth helped Fuller grow measurably in the early to late seventies. When I left the seminary we had grown from some four hundred students in the three graduate schools to over sixteen hundred, and the enrollment kept growing until its rolls showed upwards of three thousand men and women. Today, it remains the largest nondenominational school in the country.

I'm convinced God planted me at Fuller at the time when students were most receptive to our growing focus on evangelism. I was no more than a servant in that particular mix, privileged to have God's hand on me, my teaching and my life.

The rapid growth of the student body brought with it another new breed of men and women, many of whom had little or no spiritual maturity. Hundreds came without church background or exposure to congregational life and ministry. Many in my classes had almost no spiritual direction, had never been discipled, did not even know how to read the Bible for themselves or be fed by God's Word. Nor had they really gotten into prayer with any degree of consistency or knowledge. Certainly they were hungry for knowledge and fellowship. That was one of the reasons they had entered seminary. But now they found themselves in a strange new community, burdened with heavy schedules, with little opportunity to develop deep relationships in the midst of their academic pursuits. For all of us, students and teachers alike, it was always so easy to learn *about God without ever learning to know God.*

The Joy of Personal Relationships

The faculty longed to be able to give time to the students, and the young men and women needed this out-of-class nurturing. But the pressures of research, writing books, preparing lectures and grading papers made this a difficult task for most professors. When I first came to the school I expected I would have the time and energy to encourage and give counsel to students in a more intimate way than from behind a classroom lectern alone. But I, too, found I became overwhelmed by the demands of my job, which including advancing in scholarly knowledge and writing books and other curricula for classes.

I became concerned. Would I fall into the same trap I saw other faculty members falling into? In the long run, would I become so institutionalized and predictable in my approach that within a matter of a few years I would simply be there taking roll and lecturing, but not knowing the students? Fuller was—and is—blessed with a great faculty and great courses, but the perennial problem is that students often have difficulty finding themselves. There was always that creative tension that made our potential scholars wonder who they were, what they were doing and where they were headed.

An interesting research study emerged around 1975, when Thomas H. Holmes and Richard H. Rahe of the University of Washington published their scale for measuring stress associated with forty-three life-change events. These included the death of a spouse, divorce, death of a family member and so on. Too much life change in too short a time, the two researchers suggested, can create mental, spiritual and physical overload. The scale indicates that if one has a score of 100 to 300, the odds of an impending illness are raised to 51 percent. A score of 300 plus means one has an 80 percent chance of becoming seriously ill. A student in our school of psychology researched two or three of the small groups in my Foundations of Ministry class and discovered the average student was already operating at over 300 and often as high as 400, which meant there was a high probability of serious illness around the corner.

That survey made me understand the tremendous pressure under which our students were working and further helped me to emphasize the importance of sharing with each other our burdens, our stresses and our feelings. Students discovered that expressing their honest feelings— and having somebody listen to them with concern and identification— had its own marvelous healing effect. The relationships we developed because of this mutual openness enhanced all of our lives—and continues to do so to this day.

As a faculty member I already had firm biblical and theological convictions, but now I was developing an appreciation for the importance of a sensitive psychological understanding of our students as well. In one area, however, I was still less than comfortable: I did not understand the nature of *spiritual development* well enough to be able to pass it on. Slowly, however, I began to comprehend this issue and eventually had confidence enough to teach it. Before each class would begin, I was aware I was taking a crash course in virtually all the subjects I was teaching. I never entered a classroom cocksure about my ability to handle any subject matter flawlessly. I was always on the edge of my own understanding of my subject, which prevented dogmatism and encouraged the use of the Socratic form of dialogue. Questions and answers; answers and questions; questions, questions, questions . . . no answers. Such was the nature of the give and take that made student and teacher one.

Faith Renewal Teams

I learned much as a professor at Fuller, but perhaps the most critical thing God taught me was the importance of *teaming in mission* for spiritual formation and ministry. I had to learn that there is a difference between teaming for fellowship and personal growth and teaming in a common ministry in which one is out there doing it—*doing it together,* with each person part of a support team in actually fulfilling the purpose.

The following story is a good example of what I mean. During my first spring quarter at Fuller, I was invited to hold a mission at the First Presbyterian Church of San Luis Obispo. Bob Rodin, a teaching biologist at the University, had been in the Berkeley church years before and was now an elder in the San Luis Obispo church. He had a heart for missions and arranged my invitation to share with the San Luis Obispo congregation. I suggested that I would rather not do this alone but would like to bring three student couples with me. (I had already learned there was nothing more convincing of the truth of Christ in one's life than to see and hear eager young people who had chosen to forsake the appeal of money and "success" to become faithful servants of the Lord.) Dr. Rodin readily agreed with my suggestion, and together, as a team, the students went up with me on our first mission. I suggested that when we gave our witness we not share success stories about how "once I was sad, now I'm glad, once I was bad, now I'm good." Instead, I hoped we would share with our hearers that "he changed me from what I was, brought new life and purpose into my heart and mind, and I find he's with me now. However, the Lord who saved me then is now saving me from the pressures and circumstances of today. I'm still in a struggle, but God is keeping my chin above water by his grace, and we're here to tell you not success stories of radiant Christians who never have problems, but rather how we are being held together by the marvelous love and grace of Jesus Christ."

They all agreed their testimonies would go in two directions: vertically, sharing what Christ had done for us first, and then horizontally, telling what God was doing for us today in the journey of life. For this fledgling team, going out to minister for the first time, their own faith was on the line. But would their faith be strong enough to venture it? Would they risk going to an unknown place, with unknown people, and be willing to stand up and say what Christ meant to them in the struggles of seminary—to speak to the challenges of their student and personal lives?

I knew it was futile to try to fake it if there was any real desire to see the Spirit of God work. That's why we had to keep in shape spiritually, ever remaining in touch with God and with each other to demonstrate authenticity in sharing our witness.

That Friday night the members of the team gave their personal witness to some one hundred or more students from the area. The interest in their simple, straightforward approach was more than any of us had hoped for. Later when I spoke my word as follow-up, I gave an opportunity for the audience to consider the claims of Christ quietly in their hearts and make a personal response. I didn't even ask the people to raise their hands, but simply said we would be back Sunday morning and that we hoped everyone would bring two or three friends. Sunday morning two more members of the team gave their witness in what we now called "twofold dimensions," vertical and horizontal. Right with God and right together with brothers and sisters. "Get right, get together, and get going" was Sam Shoemaker's great formula, which we were really working at the time.

Many were back, some with friends along. In that setting, I didn't hesitate to invite members of the audience to step forward in a public confession for Christ, even though it really stunned the old members of the church because they had never seen anything like this in their lives. It even surprised the members of the team. But what amazed them most was the riveting impact of their testimony: a dozen or more students and two or three adults actually came forward as seekers.

On our return trip to Pasadena, they were some of the most excited students I've ever been with. Jon Wilson, who had another year to go, said, "Dr. Munger, we've got to do this some more!" And indeed we did. While driving back to campus we discussed the idea of putting together not a gospel team, but something we would call a Faith Renewal Team. We postulated that a team member couldn't bring faith with him on the road if he didn't already have it. But faith could be renewed if a man or woman was already a believer.

The name stuck, and the Faith Renewal Team was born. The idea of the team effort was not only to quicken the soul of the individual team member but also to quicken the life of the congregation. Our simple message was that through Christ we have new life, a new sense of love, and above all a companion and Lord who is leading us on our journey and giving us unspeakable joy.

That trip to San Luis Obispo was the beginning of a team movement at Fuller that helped shape the lives of hundreds of young seminarians in the years ahead. The following fall Jon Wilson brought together another six couples, mature seniors, eager to get out and do something for God. They weren't satisfied with a mundane, routine job in a church that would not give them the fresh experience of this type of teaming. They too became part of our growing group. Teaming in ministry was for them, and for hundreds more, a simple, honest experience of the great hope that was within them. The principles of teaming stayed practical and alive, because the students made the conscious commitment to remain accountable to one another. They also made the commitment to speak openly of their struggles every time they spoke, and to rely on the support of the team as they shared their struggles as well as their victories. It was *koinōnia* in its truest form.

While the team grew in love for the Lord and for each other, the avowed intent of our renewal effort was to minister to local congregations. Our purpose was to quicken an awareness in evangelism and to be God's instruments to help renew the faith of people in the church. As a team we did our best to model what a Christian relationship could really be. God always seemed to use us to the degree to which we practiced our relationships during the week—loving one another at every opportunity, being brothers and sisters to one another and caring for each other, helping each other in our doubts, our fears and even our finances. One team member wrecked his car on his weekly commute to work in a local church. Without saying a word to anyone publicly, the six people on his team collected enough of their little savings to help him buy a used car which got him through to the end of the school year. That was our team in action. They spoke what they believed and lived what they were imparting to others.

I often used one little "show and tell" technique to help the team understand what really happens when we do—and do not—work together. I would take a styrofoam cup, punch several holes in it and then pour a generous amount of water into it. Obviously, water poured out from all sides and the cup quickly emptied. Then I punched holes in another cup in like manner. This time, I put the second cup into the first one and filled it with water. An amazing thing happened. Water still came out, but not with the same rate of flow. Then I took a third, fourth and a fifth cup, all duly punched full of holes. And by now you know the result. The holes no longer had the same effect. While water came out freely when one cup was on its own, no water came out when the cups were fitted closely together. That's what teaming was—and is—all about. We were always better off *together* than when we were separate.

The amazing thing about this team effort is that I can think of only one person who dropped out in all the ten years I worked with them. When one figures our Faith Renewal Teams brought together more than 250 students over a decade, that's not a bad average. One person died of cancer during our time together, and that was a tragedy we all had to deal with—something a psychologist would call material for our spiritual and emotional growth. But that, too, was a bonding experience for the team and for myself. As always, the team was there, ready and able to be God's men and women at a time of great need. One of our hallmarks was 1 John 4:11: "Since God so loved us, we also ought to love one another."

While our little group of committed seminarians was an encouragement to others, the greatest impact of the team ministry was what it did for the members themselves. I thought it was by far the best thing God allowed me to do at Fuller in leadership development. I think those who were with us would say, almost to a person, that they learned as much about leadership development and spiritual resources in that team experience as they did in any of their other courses in seminary. Today, many of those students continue to carry the spirit of the team in their ministries in this country and around the world.

I suppose if I were starting all over mentoring team members today, I would probably add some of the principles from the Twelve Steps of Alcoholics Anonymous. Why? Because I'm now convinced that we are all basically severely addicted. We're addicted to sin and to the dominant desire of self to play the role of God. It's hard for us to be submissive to Christ as Lord and do what we know very well he asks us to. The old "flesh" has a way of imposing itself on us, dominating us, crushing us. And for that reason we need to treat the "lust of the flesh, the lust of the eyes and the pride of life" as an addiction. I believe a modern-day faith renewal team could take the principles of Alcoholics Anonymous and put them to good use in the Master's service wherever they might serve—in the home, as small group leaders, as pastors or as church administrators.

I knew one thing for sure: our committed team members would never again go it alone in ministry. They learned what leaders today need to learn: *teaming is a cure for burnout and a sense of spiritual failure.* Teaming keeps one honest. Teaming keeps one humble. Teaming keeps one's perspective on the right track. Teaming provides fellowship. Teaming means you are never alone. For these reasons, those in or aspiring to leadership positions today simply *must* understand and implement the principles of a team. I do not believe that today's pastors can thrive—or even survive—as leaders without it.

For me, now almost two decades later, these principles continue to be alive in my own life. Whatever our ministry may be, we shoot ourselves in the foot if we insist on doing it all alone.

We need to take a fresh look at the life of Jesus and remember that he worked with a team! He not only trusted his disciples—his laity—but he spent time with them talking, eating, working, traveling. They were inseparable. Jesus gave his team special attention and asked them questions so they would give him feedback to show whether they grasped the full scope of his teaching. He taught them together, and he also taught them one at a time. He saw each person as a different personality and spoke to that disciple with deep sensitivity. Jesus was so much more than a quiet role model. He got involved with his team and gave them explicit instructions. As the team members would then go out on a mission two by two, he told them what to take, what to do and *how* to do it. That's involvement. Thank God our Faith Renewal Team members learned these same solid principles over the years, as we created a program that would meet *our* needs, would touch the lives of others and could be duplicated in the hearts of those we met.

I close this chapter—and this book—with a few paragraphs from letters I have received from some of these team member over the years. While they express their appreciation for my being their mentor, they give God the ultimate glory for how the Faith Renewal Team helped in the *formation* of their lives and ministries.

On the Faith Renewal Team I learned to love and learned how to let others love me. It was because of this love, acceptance and the close communion with others that the self-erected barriers within me began to crumble and I became more real. Further, I came to better understand the meaning of the Church universal: to discover there were others in churches beyond my small world who love Jesus Christ as much as I love him.—Glory Hees

What a wonderful opportunity it was to be on the team. We really could, in the midst of actual ministry, explore and try out our gifts. We worked together as a body. How I trembled from fear as I stood in front of those churches, but my team members supported me in prayer.—Karen Lann

"Remember Jesus Christ," you said to me at my service of installation . . . and I will, because through you Jesus Christ has come alive to me in a way I had never known before. I have laughed with you, cried with you, prayed, preached and testified with you, and there has never been a man this side of heaven I have felt more love from than you. I look forward to an eternity together as your brother in Christ.—Doug Millham

Dr. Munger first started inviting a few couples to accompany him on weekend speaking engagements. As a team we set up entire renewal weekends. We started on Friday nights with meetings in small groups in homes led by one of our couples. We would have special classes on Saturday morning for spiritual growth and discussion, and culminate the weekend with participation in the Sunday morning worship service. Each Wednesday night we would meet in a home for a potluck supper and share our lives—the struggles, the pains, the victories, the answered prayers. Then we would minister to each other in prayer and plan the next weekend. Dr. Bob was one of the team, leading from behind, lifting from below, helping us to be our best for God. The principles learned those twenty-five years ago I have used to turn one church around, and I'm slowly turning around another.—Jon Wilson

As a member of the Faith Renewal Team for two years, it was my privilege to work at your side as team leader and captain. You taught me during those years to pray, to accept one another, to listen, to express our faith, and how to help people in the local church. Our marriage was strengthened, our ministry deepened.—Jim Hazlett

Thank you, dear friends, for your words of encouragement. It is you who encouraged me. It is you who kept me on the path of servant ministry. It is you who have taken the torch of Christ's love to those who are lost at home and abroad. And while sickness and death will ultimately take members of our team from each other here on earth, let's remember that we will have an eternity to replay our experiences and relive the lives we so earnestly committed to the Father. Thank you for being such a wonderful part of my journey—one that truly will never end.

EPILOGUE
The
Journey
Never Ends

Even during the long months of producing this manuscript, I felt God at work in my life as I reflected back upon my sometimes tumultuous, sometimes placid voyage with my Captain, Savior and Friend. In retrospect it does seem I've struggled more in the foamy white water and violent waves than taken silent refuge in quiet harbors of ministry. The entire experience of my life as a servant leader has been a venture and an adventure.

At UC-Berkeley my faith started out as a question mark, to grow into ultimate certainty with an acquaintance who became a Friend, and who then became my Captain. For me the most powerful awareness was that the more I got to know him, the more I desired to serve him. I had always wanted a real friend, and that is exactly what Jesus became—and continues to be to me today.

For today's Christian leaders, who are forced to meet unbelievably difficult situations as they move into the twenty-first century, I covet this same deep relationship with Jesus Christ. Nonstop activity for the Lord

can be devastating if there is not the counterbalance of quiet solace—
taking time to be with one's Friend and Captain. I learned this lesson
the hard way, and while I suppose it's true that we all have to learn our
own life lessons, I trust my experiences as related in this book will at
least send up a caution signal to those who are gifted in the aggressive
side of ministry but perhaps less aware of the crucial importance of
spending time alone with the Captain.

I am eternally grateful for the many teachers, professors, mentors and
parishioners who have helped me study the message, learn it and appreciate its ramifications. These friends helped me learn to navigate the
rough rapids and take the trial runs in my vocation as player-coach.

To the many stalwarts of the faith whose paths I crossed I also owe
a debt of gratitude for teaching me the three great themes of ministry:
*the importance of prayer, the vitality of evangelism and the absolute
essential of mission.* Once I began to grasp the importance of this tripod
of ministry, each became constantly validated in real-life situations. The
principles worked for me, are still working for me and will also work
for you. That is why I hope that you see them as *certainties* rather than
possibilities. When you do, you will be more than fit for your own
journey. Not that you will no longer experience doubts, fears or temptations, but you will now know beyond the shadow of a doubt that your
Captain and Friend will always be at your side, not judging or carping,
but tenderly, graciously loving you because that is his nature.

The thing I think I've learned most confidently in my years of sharing
the gospel is that I was not so much entrusted with leadership as I was
with servanthood. A true leader is a servant. A real leader leads from
below—lifting, encouraging, speaking words of comfort and challenge.
During my ten years at Fuller Seminary I was grateful for the opportunities God gave me to do my best to be a servant leader. While I may
have been instrumental in bringing people to faith, commitment and
maturing throughout my early ministry, it was those years at Fuller
where it all seemed to come together.

And it carried on even after I retired from Fuller and ventured to the Menlo Park Presbyterian Church, where I served as one of the associate pastors for seven years. There the supremacy of love was the dominant theme. It was a ministry that called for love, love and more love—and I thanked God daily that he had given me the opportunity to explore the full range of those possibilities. The guidelines I'd learned on my long journey still worked.

God's guidelines *always* work. The various areas of practical ministry I participated in at Moody and Princeton were still what people wanted and craved. But now I was older, hopefully wiser, and even more able to reach out to feel and appreciate the needs of others. Now I know for certain that the journey never ends. I'm still learning so much, and God continually gives me fresh new insights. In retirement, the pace has become slower and more voluntary, but nevertheless real. My commitment to my Captain and Friend has not wavered.

As I realize that I've lived many lives in one lifetime, I am learning the importance of unceasing praise to the glory of God. 2 Corinthians 4:6 says it best: "For God, who said, 'Let light shine out of darkness,' made his light shine in our hearts to give us the light of the knowledge of the glory of God in the face of Jesus Christ." For this journey that never ends I am grateful beyond measure. And I will be forever grateful for my helpmeet, Edie, to whom I am so indebted for all she has done and continues to do for me. With my Captain and Friend and with Edie, what more could this preacher want, anyway!

God bless you, dear reader, and may our Savior and Lord become *your* Captain and Friend from now throughout eternity, as you experience your own journey that never ends.